Praise for *Inspire Greatness*

"It's not often that a business book completely disrupts the status quo. *Inspire Greatness* does exactly that. In this engaging book you'll discover a compelling explanation for why the average levels of employee engagement and motivation haven't improved in more than 20 years, along with an innovative solution that will help you and your organization to improve and sustain employee engagement and performance. If you are a leader of people, the learning moments shared in *Inspire Greatness* are must-reads!"

—Garry Ridge, Chairman Emeritus, WD-40
Company, and The Culture Coach

"*Inspire Greatness* presents an innovative, systematic approach to developing highly engaged and motivated employees. With practical strategies and actionable steps, Matt Tenney offers a path any leader can follow to consistently inspire and empower individuals to reach their full potential. This transformative guide equips leaders and leadership teams with a process and tools for building a sustainable, high-performance culture that drives organizational success and helps employees thrive."

—Skip Prichard, CEO, OCLC, Inc., and Author, *The Book of Mistakes: 9 Secrets to Creating a Successful Future*

"In *Inspire Greatness*, Matt Tenney has done an exceptional job of presenting a clear, concise, and compelling game plan to improve employee engagement, company culture, and organizational success. His narrative style is a standout feature, making this book an engaging read that avoids overwhelming the reader with complex terminology. Instead, it offers straightforward explanations and real-life examples of what drives human behavior and helps managers unleash discretionary effort. I highly recommend this book to any leader who wants to more consistently serve team members and inspire peak performance."

—Lou Gizzarelli, President, Quadient Canada

"*Inspire Greatness* is a groundbreaking book on employee motivation and engagement. Matt Tenney highlights the importance of routinely executing often-overlooked fundamentals of leadership and includes a practical road map for being a leader who consistently inspires high levels of performance. *Inspire Greatness* is a must-read for all leaders—from the front line to the C-Suite—who want to be better leaders of teams and improve business results."

—Mark Smith, Executive Director, Global Talent,
The Kraft Heinz Company

"In *Inspire Greatness*, Matt Tenney shares an 'engagement acceleration formula' that can be easily scaled across an entire organization. I strongly recommend this insightful book to all leaders, especially those looking to improve sales by helping sales managers be better coaches and leaders of fast-growing start-ups, which need a repeatable process for leadership development to ensure they maintain a strong culture during periods of rapid growth."

—Mark Roberge, Cofounder, Stage 2 Capital; Senior Lecturer, Harvard Business School; Founding CRO, HubSpot; and Bestselling Author, *The Sales Acceleration Formula*

"*Inspire Greatness* is an inspirational and thought-provoking book. Matt Tenney offers valuable insights and practical wisdom on how to lead in a way that makes a positive impact on the performance, growth, and well-being of team members. Matt's engaging storytelling and real-world examples will empower you to cultivate a culture of greatness in your team and your organization. *Inspire Greatness* is a must-read for anyone looking to be more effective as a leader while also finding deeper meaning and fulfillment at work. Using Matt's simple four-step approach, you'll learn how to create simple habits for consistently bringing out the best in the people you lead."

—Alyssa Thach, Cofounder and CEO, Pierpoint International

"*Inspire Greatness* should become mandatory reading for every business leader in every industry. Matt Tenney has distilled the essence of leadership to *the* single most important responsibility that must be at the top of every leader's job description: 'to inspire greatness in one's team by serving as a coach who helps others to be happy, great human beings, who do great work.' I wish Matt had written this book forty years ago, when I first started in business. It would have helped me avoid the costly mistakes I made while managing my team of 400 staff. This is not just another philosophical leadership book, but is jam-packed with research, unforgettable examples, and prescriptive action plans that when implemented will significantly elevate any company's engagement, productivity, and profits."

—Russell M. Kern, CEO, Kern and Partners, and Founder and former CEO, Kern Agency, An Omnicom Company

"*Inspire Greatness* is an engaging, page-turner of a book that includes a very innovative approach to employee motivation and engagement. We've applied the guidance Matt offers in this book to help us increase employee engagement, dramatically reduce employee turnover, and navigate the uncharted territory of being the first national law firm to implement a four-day workweek for both attorneys and staff. I highly recommend this book!"

—Steve Fields, Founder and CEO, Fields Law Firm

"In the crowded field of leadership development books, *Inspire Greatness* stands out and shines. Matt Tenney offers a unique approach for improving employee motivation and engagement that is both simple and much more effective than the traditional approach. I strongly recommend this book to any leader who would like a repeatable process for quickly and sustainably improving both the performance and well-being of managers and team members."

—Craig Simpkins, Global Leader, Finance, Early
Talent Development, Johnson Controls

"In the ever-evolving landscape of human resources (HR), finding strategies to effectively motivate employees is a constant pursuit. This book brilliantly addresses this challenge with an approach that is both practical and insightful.

As Vice President of Human Resources, I am always on the lookout for resources that provide actionable solutions to enhance employee engagement and drive organizational success. *Inspire Greatness* delivers precisely that. The author's commitment to simplicity, repeatability, and scalability resonates deeply with HR professionals like me, who are seeking sustainable methods to inspire and empower their leaders.

What sets this book apart is its emphasis on a process that is not only grounded in research and best practices but also adaptable to various industries and company sizes. The real-world examples and case studies provide invaluable context, making the strategies easy to grasp and implement.

Inspire Greatness is a must-read for HR leaders, managers, and anyone passionate about cultivating a thriving workplace culture. Matt Tenney's expertise and passion for employee motivation shine through, offering a comprehensive guide that will undoubtedly become a cornerstone for HR professionals and leaders seeking to make a meaningful impact.

I wholeheartedly recommend *Inspire Greatness* as a game-changing addition to the toolkit of anyone invested in creating a motivated, engaged, and high-performing workforce."

—Maryana Sinishtay, Vice President of Human Resources,
Diamond Properties & Diamond Hospitality Group

"I love this book! Matt Tenney offers a simple, practical path to consistently closing the gap between who we aspire to be as leaders and how we actually show up each day. *Inspire Greatness* is the best book I have read on the topic of effectively serving and bringing out the best in team members, and it is a must-read for any modern leader."

—Felix Frowein, Senior Vice President, Global
Consumer Fragrances at dsm-firmenich

"Groundbreaking and actionable, *Inspire Greatness* is a master class in leadership. It's a data-driven, no-nonsense guide that will transform managers into inspirational leaders. In a world filled with leadership manuals, *Inspire Greatness* stands out as a must-read."

—Derick Dickens, Senior Vice President of
Training, Civic Federal Credit Union

INSPIRE GREATNESS

Also by Matt Tenney

Serve to Be Great: Leadership Lessons from a Prison,
a Monastery, and a Boardroom

The Mindfulness Edge: How to Rewire Your Brain for Leadership
and Personal Excellence Without Adding to Your Schedule

INSPIRE GREATNESS

How to Motivate Employees with a Simple, Repeatable, Scalable Process

MATT TENNEY

Matt Holt Books
An Imprint of BenBella Books, Inc.
Dallas, TX

Matt Holt is an imprint of BenBella Books, Inc.
10440 N. Central Expressway
Suite 800
Dallas, TX 75231
benbellabooks.com
Send feedback to feedback@benbellabooks.com

BenBella and *Matt Holt* are federally registered trademarks.

Printed in the United States of America
10 9 8 7 6 5 4 3 2 1

Library of Congress Control Number: 2023045213
ISBN 9781637745076 (hardcover)
ISBN 9781637745083 (electronic)

Editing by Katie Dickman
Copyediting by Michael Fedison
Proofreading by Lisa Story and Denise Pangia
Text design and composition by PerfecType, Nashville, TN
Cover design by Brigid Pearson
Cover image © Shutterstock / pixssa
Printed by Lake Book Manufacturing

This book is dedicated to you. May it help you to be a highly effective leader who inspires greatness in others, and to realize deep meaning and fulfillment in your work.

CONTENTS

INTRODUCTION

As of this writing, a search on Amazon.com for "leadership books" yields over sixty thousand results. Could there possibly be anything new to say on this subject?

I certainly hope there is because, as you'll discover in chapter one of this book, research from the Gallup organization shows that, on average, we leaders have not improved our ability to lead people at all over the last twenty years. Perhaps this is one reason people keep writing leadership books.

I believe another reason so many books have been written on this topic is that leadership is thought of as an *art*, not a *science*. There are many different leadership styles, and even more opinions regarding which style will yield the best results. And when leadership principles and ideas are shared, they tend to not be shared as part of a holistic, systematic approach that any leader could apply, regardless of one's leadership style or natural ability, to more consistently drive high levels of performance.

What if there was an *algorithm*, a repeatable process, based on decades of research on what motivates employees, that any leader could follow to consistently bring out the best in her team?

This is a question I've wrestled with for the last decade, since the publication of my first book, *Serve to Be Great: Leadership Lessons from a Prison, a Monastery, and a Boardroom*. My intent with that book was to inspire people to think differently about leadership and focus more on taking good care of employees.

Apparently, there is a strong appetite for this type of message. The book has done well and, over the last ten years, I've been invited to deliver hundreds of keynote speeches and training programs for universities, associations, midsize businesses you've probably never heard of, and some of the most recognizable companies in the world, like Keller Williams, Marriott, and Salesforce.

Although I do agree that there is value to programs that inspire people to think differently, and I truly enjoy delivering keynotes and training programs, something has been missing for me over the last ten years. I aspire to make even more of an impact by helping people transform ideas into new behaviors that become new habits.

Thus, over the past ten years, I have spent much of my time searching for a repeatable process leaders could use to create lasting behavior changes that consistently drive high levels of employee engagement and retention.

In 2021, while researching employee engagement survey practices, I stumbled upon a key insight that solves the most important problems regarding both leadership development and employee engagement. Much to my surprise, this insight also resulted in the discovery of a simple, repeatable, scalable process that any leader can follow, regardless of one's leadership style or natural leadership ability, to transform ideas into lasting behaviors that are proven to increase employee engagement.

This process is supported by decades of research on what the most successful leaders, teams, and organizations do to create high levels of employee motivation and engagement. And it has been further refined by clients ranging from small businesses to big tech to the Fortune 100, as well as in the two companies I've founded in the last five years.

In Part 1 of this book, you'll learn the simple, four-step process that I discovered for consistently bringing out the best in team members. And if you're an executive (a leader of leaders), or a human resources or people operations professional, you'll discover how to apply this powerful process to build and scale an entire leadership team that creates consistently high levels of employee engagement, attracts and retains top talent, and drives sustainable high performance.

In Part 2, you'll discover simple behaviors for consistently bringing out the best in team members and how to use the process outlined in Part 1 to transform what you read into lasting habits.

I certainly don't think this is the only book you should ever read on leadership. There are many excellent books on leadership that I believe can be very helpful.

However, I am very confident that this book will help you see leadership as less of an *art* and more of a *science*. It will help you transform the ideas you learn in this book (and in other leadership books) into meaningful, lasting behaviors by applying a simple, repeatable, scalable process that empowers you and the other leaders in your organization to consistently inspire greatness in your team members.

PART 1

A Simple, Repeatable, Scalable Process for Consistently Bringing Out the Best in Your Team Members

1

Employee Engagement

One of the Greatest Mysteries in Business

Jennifer is a young, charismatic woman with lots of energy. She is one of the apparently rare people who seem to be able to do it all. She is extremely organized, has an incredible work ethic, and also deeply cares about people.

This combination of traits helped her advance very quickly in her career in people operations (people ops), earning her numerous promotions in just a few years, and an offer to take on a high-level role as a regional director of human resources (HR). Jennifer accepted the offer and was very excited to jump right into her new role. Her goal was to make a noticeable impact in her first sixty days.

She was well aware that there was a lot of work to be done, but this is what Jennifer lives for. Her primary motivator is making an impact, and she was very confident that there was tremendous untapped potential for the company and the nearly nine hundred employees she served.

Her priority was to reduce employee turnover at the company, which had reached a staggering 55 percent. This was much higher than the average turnover rate for their industry.

She knew that after accounting for the costs of hiring and lost team productivity, the Gallup organization estimates the true cost of losing one mid-level employee is approximately the annual salary of that employee. So, she used a simple formula for determining the true cost of turnover for the company (Number of Employees × Average Non-C-Suite Salary × Turnover Rate), and calculated that turnover was costing the company over $28 million per year. She realized that just getting the turnover rate down to the industry average of 25 percent would save her company over $15 million per year.

One morning, after just a few weeks with the company, she was reading an exit interview conducted with an employee who had recently left. The interview provided some helpful clues for understanding the cause of the high turnover at the company.

David, the subject of the interview, was a dream employee. He was a top performer. He had already been promoted twice and was being compensated very well for his position, earning about $125,000 per year.

Then, after three years with the company, he unexpectedly gave his two weeks' notice and left to go work for a competitor. Apparently, the competitor offered him just $5,000 more than his salary at Jennifer's company. Jennifer was almost certain that David didn't leave for a 4 percent pay raise.

Yet, this was a pretty common scenario at the company. Many employees said the reason they left was pay, but the pay increases were negligible. Jennifer knew that the real issue was the company culture.

Research published in *MIT Sloan Management Review* supported her diagnosis. The study analyzed thirty-four million online employee profiles to identify US workers who left their employer for any reason during a six-month period in 2021. According to the authors, "A toxic corporate culture is by far the strongest predictor of industry-adjusted attrition and is 10 times more important than compensation in predicting turnover."

Although she didn't think the culture at her new company was truly toxic, she knew there was a lot of room for improvement. Jennifer quickly developed a plan for improving the culture, starting with an employee engagement survey.

She knew that company culture, employee engagement, and employee retention are all very tightly correlated. She also knew that the issues uncovered with an employee engagement survey should help her take the actions necessary to improve the culture and reduce turnover.

Her team put a lot of work into preparing for the survey, launching the survey, poring through the results, and formulating a plan for addressing the issues they identified. Unfortunately, the survey questions didn't translate well into easily actionable items. So, it took the HR team a couple hundred hours, spread out over three months, to create their plan.

It was clear from the survey results that most of the issues that needed to be addressed revolved around how well managers were leading their team members. So, Jennifer suggested to senior leaders that the organization invest in leadership development for all managers. The senior leadership team was motivated to reduce the $28 million cost of turnover, and agreed to invest in leadership training. However, the budget for the training was limited, and wouldn't be available for at least three months.

The HR team did the best they could given the time and budget constraints. The leadership development training consisted of a few half-day workshops that occurred seven months after the survey from the previous year. The team was excited and optimistic that helping managers grow would make a significant impact.

The workshops seemed to be a hit. The feedback from the managers was almost all positive.

Five months after all the managers had attended the workshops, a year after the previous survey, Jennifer looked at the turnover numbers. Her heart nearly broke. Annual turnover had actually *increased* to 58 percent.

Not long after that, her team conducted the second annual employee engagement survey. According to the survey, employee engagement had actually become worse, too.

Sadly, Jennifer's story is not unique. In fact, some variation of this story is the norm, not the exception.

The Power of Engaged Employees

Although the term "employee engagement" was first used in the 1990s, the concept has existed for as long as people have led teams. An engaged employee is an employee who is emotionally invested in her work and willing to give discretionary effort. In other words, an engaged employee is a motivated employee who is willing to go the extra mile to do great work and accomplish the mission.

Clearly, common sense would suggest that the more motivated, or engaged, employees there are in an organization, the better the performance of the organization; and the more unmotivated employees there are, the worse the performance. And, thanks to the Gallup organization, there is now a very large body of research quantifying the benefits of high levels of employee engagement, and the negative impact of unmotivated employees.

Below are just a few areas where Gallup routinely finds that companies in the top 25 percent of employee engagement levels outperform those in the bottom 25 percent:

- Approximately 81 percent lower absenteeism
- Approximately 30 percent better employee retention
- Ten percent better customer loyalty/engagement
- Approximately 18 percent better sales
- Approximately 23 percent higher profitability

Also, a broad meta-analysis Gallup conducted of employee engagement research found that companies with highly engaged workforces outperform their less-engaged peers by an incredible 147 percent in earnings per share. Gallup estimates that low employee engagement costs US businesses $500 billion annually and costs the global economy $7.8 trillion annually.

This is a good spot to pause and reflect for a moment. If a good number of your team members aren't highly motivated, how much is it costing your team or organization?

The Mystery of Employee Engagement

Employee engagement has been formally measured by the Gallup organization since the year 2000. As you may be aware, when Gallup first started measuring employee engagement, the numbers were terrible. In 2001, in the US, only 30 percent—roughly one out of three employees—were engaged at work. The numbers outside the US were significantly worse.

The vast majority of employees were either not engaged, which means they were just showing up for the paycheck and doing the bare minimum that's needed to keep their jobs, or they were *actively disengaged*, which means that they were actually undermining the performance of the rest of their teams and organizations.

Fortunately, we have an abundance of research conducted over the last fifty years that has provided very clear evidence for exactly what motivates employees and drives employee engagement in the workplace. This research is public knowledge, available to everyone. And, over the last twenty years, US companies alone have spent hundreds of billions of dollars on surveys and training programs trying to improve employee engagement in the workplace.

What types of results have we seen with this extremely powerful combination of knowing exactly what drives employee engagement and an enormous amount of resources being applied to increasing employee engagement? None.

That's right. We have seen no statistically significant increase in the average levels of employee engagement in the last twenty years. As of this writing in 2023, in the US, the average level of employee engagement is still hovering slightly below one out of three (32 percent). And the numbers are still worse outside the US.

Of course, this begs the question:

Why haven't we been able to improve employee engagement to any significant degree in the last twenty years despite knowing exactly what drives employee engagement and applying massive amounts of resources toward increasing employee engagement?

Why Employee Engagement Hasn't Improved in Twenty Years

In 2021, while researching employee engagement survey practices, I stumbled upon the answer to the question above. I discovered that there are three persistent and extremely important issues, which, together, have resulted in the average levels of employee engagement not improving at all over the last twenty years:

1. Employee engagement is perceived, incorrectly, as an "HR thing" that can be improved with perks and benefits. The result is that engagement initiatives tend to be separated by time and/ or function from leadership development initiatives.

   However, according to research from Gallup, at least 70 percent of employee engagement and retention is driven by direct managers. In order to quickly and sustainably improve employee engagement and retention, there needs to be a heavy focus on leadership development, and leadership development needs to be tightly synchronized with efforts to measure and improve employee engagement.

2. Unfortunately, even when leadership training is offered, research suggests that as much as 85–90 percent of it fails to create any lasting improvements.

   For leadership training to produce a return on investment, it can't just be an information transfer. Leadership training needs to effectively build new habits that stick, and that are proven to improve engagement and retention and drive sustainable high performance.

3. The act of measuring employee engagement almost always has a negative impact on trust in leadership, and thus on employee engagement and retention. The typical annual survey process often actually does more harm than good, primarily because it results in long time gaps between feedback and meaningful action in response to that feedback.

   Employee feedback needs to be gathered in a way that makes it easy to quickly respond to the feedback. This makes it possible to get feedback and measure engagement in a way that, in and of itself, *builds* confidence and trust in leadership, and improves employee engagement and retention.

It is *extremely important* to note that the primary reason employee engagement hasn't improved in the last twenty years is that *all three* of these issues are intimately interconnected. There have been attempts to solve the issues above separately. However, in order to finally solve the puzzle of employee engagement, and see significant, sustainable improvements in engagement levels, *all three* of the issues above need to be resolved at the same time.

It was only when I saw how the three issues above work together (or have failed to work together over the last two decades) that the solution to the problem became obvious. And the simple, four-step process that I discovered (and is supported by decades of research on employee engagement) can be applied by any leader to consistently drive high levels of engagement and performance on her team. You'll learn this four-step process in this book.

If you're an executive (a leader of leaders), or an HR or people ops professional, you'll discover how to apply this powerful process to build and scale an entire leadership team that creates consistently high levels of employee engagement, attracts and retains top talent, and drives sustainable high performance.

Let's start with the foundational issue, the very common misperception that employee engagement is an "HR thing." Ironically, this misperception is fueled in part by the illusion of being known as a "best place to work."

The Illusion of Being a "Best Place to Work"

Ana is one of the smartest, most driven people I have met. She was born to extremely hardworking parents in Mexico City, where hard work is ingrained in the culture. Ana's work ethic is paired with an intense curiosity and excellent listening skills, and her resume is filled with positions at well-known tech companies that make her a constant target of recruiters trying to entice her to come work for the companies they represent.

A few years ago, a company was able to successfully pull her away from one of the most well-known tech giants in the world, known for being among the best places to work. When I asked Ana about why she would leave such a well-known company with a great culture, her answer surprised me.

She said, "The culture there is an illusion. Many teams inside the company are actually toxic."

How does this happen?

Over the last twenty years or so, an incredible body of work has been created around the importance of having a "great place to work." There are now a number of lists that rank the best places to work in a wide range of categories.

On the whole, this has been extremely important work that has inspired many leaders to make it a top priority to create a workplace that people actually enjoy being a part of. Thanks in large part to this effort, it is now widely known that employee experience, including the degree to which employees are happy, is a key element of long-term organizational success.

Unfortunately, what many people take away from these "best place to work" lists are things like benefits and perks, such as a cool office space with foosball tables, free food, and a gym. Although perks and benefits can be very effective for attracting people to an organization, with a few exceptions, they are not effective at driving employee engagement over the long term, unless more important needs are also met, which you'll learn more about soon. In fact, perks and benefits can actually hurt employee engagement when more important needs aren't met, especially when employees perceive the perks and benefits and office space to be part of a *quid pro quo*.

Ana's story is not unique. I have spoken with many employees who used to work at well-known tech companies that win "best place to work" awards—and have amazing perks and benefits—who have told me that their company culture was actually pretty toxic. They felt that leaders saw them as commodities and that there was an expectation that they should work around seventy to eighty hours per week in reciprocity for all the perks and benefits they were given. Most of these employees wanted to leave as soon as possible, and only stayed at these organizations long enough to add a well-known tech company to their resumes.

Perks and benefits have much more to do with employee *satisfaction* than they do with employee *engagement*. It is partly due to "best place to work" lists that people use employee satisfaction and employee engagement interchangeably. Although employee satisfaction is certainly a component of employee engagement, it is extremely important to make a clear distinction between these two terms.

Satisfied employees are employees who really like their workplace. Satisfied employees tend to stick around a long time because of the nice perks and benefits. At first glance this seems like a really good thing.

However, employees may be very satisfied, but not *engaged*. In other words, they may not be high performers who are emotionally invested in accomplishing the mission of the team or organization, and thereby very unlikely to go the extra mile. Having large numbers of *satisfied* employees who are not *engaged* can actually be detrimental to an organization.

If an organization has a large number of employees who are essentially doing the bare minimum to keep their jobs but are sticking around for a long time, a culture of mediocrity can easily form. A culture of mediocrity can have devastating effects on organizational performance, and can repel highly talented, highly engaged people.

The realization that benefits and perks are not effective in and of themselves for sustaining high levels of engagement and retention is actually very good news! Perks and benefits are expensive. Most leaders and organizations can't afford to compete on those factors. However, any leader or organization can execute the powerful, four-step process you're going to learn in this book.

Employee Engagement Isn't an "HR Thing"

Another negative side effect of this illusion of what it means to be a "best place to work" is that it results in thinking of workplace culture, and employee engagement and retention, as "HR things."

In small companies, many CEOs dream of the day they can hire a true HR director so that they can improve the workplace culture. In large companies, there seems to be a pervasive notion that leaders can go to HR and ask them to sprinkle some type of "magic HR fairy dust" on their workplace, and this is going to somehow miraculously create a sustainable, high-performance culture with high levels of employee engagement and retention.

This idea that HR is ultimately responsible for employee engagement and retention has devastating consequences. When employee engagement is viewed exclusively as an "HR thing," it tends to be treated by other leaders as a sort of "project," with a clear beginning and ending, that is separate from leadership development efforts. And when employee engagement is viewed as a time-bound project that is separate from leadership development efforts, the process of trying to improve employee engagement is inherently flawed, because at least 70 percent of employee engagement is driven by direct managers.

In order to be successful at creating and sustaining high levels of employee engagement, leadership development and employee engagement efforts must be synchronized as tightly as possible. Thus, the first and foundational step for improving employee engagement, and building and scaling a high-performance culture that attracts and retains top talent, is to resolve the first of the three issues outlined earlier.

The perception that employee engagement is an "HR thing"—driven primarily by perks and benefits—must be changed. Leaders at all levels need to realize that although the HR / people ops team is an extremely important partner in the efforts to drive employee engagement and retention, employee engagement is not an "HR thing."

Ultimately, employee engagement is a "leadership thing."

2

The Primary Job of a Leader

Australia is known for having much friendlier and more naturally helpful people than most Western nations. Although I haven't had the opportunity to get to know too many Australians very well, I have personally never met an Australian I didn't like.

Australia is also known for being very "macho," strongly valuing traditionally masculine traits. Researchers have quantified, to some degree, just how macho Australian society is. One study, for instance, found that Australian men were ranked as the second most misogynistic cohort of the thirty nations studied.

As in other macho countries, fathers tend to focus on encouraging their children to accomplish big things and to be "winners," while mothers tend to focus on encouraging their children to be good human beings.

But in the home in Sydney where Garry Ridge grew up, the traditional tendencies of parents were almost entirely reversed. It was his mother who was the determined, "you can climb any mountain" type, who instilled in him the values of hard work and never giving up. And it was Garry's father who was much more concerned about Garry's character. Garry's father spent most of his energy encouraging Garry to do things the right way, and to treat people with kindness and respect.

In addition to exposure to nontraditional encouragement from parents, Garry was also exposed to nontraditional sibling relationships. He was the youngest of three children. And, he wasn't the youngest by a little bit. His nearest sibling was twelve years older than him.

From the time of his earliest childhood memories, Garry was surrounded by adults. As a result, he received a lot of attention and felt truly cared for by the people in his home, which helped him realize the importance of caring for others. The first time I spoke with Garry, I immediately felt important, and that he cared about me. When speaking with Garry, he conveys a subtle, caring smile that exudes warmness.

Being a very caring teenage male didn't really fit the macho norms of Australian society. Nor did Garry's lack of athleticism. Garry learned early on that he wasn't good at sports, so he stopped playing them. Because he didn't fit the traditional norms, during his teenage years, Garry wasn't very popular with girls and didn't spend much time on the social scene.

Since many people associate leadership ability with traditional macho traits, like taking charge and telling people to "come follow me," Garry's childhood peers apparently didn't envision him as a "natural born leader." None of Garry's classmates voted him "Most likely to be a leader one day." But Garry's unique upbringing may have actually given him an unfair advantage and created a powerful foundation for later success as a business leader.

While his peers were spending time playing sports and dating, Garry started working and learning about business. In one of his early jobs, he was fortunate enough to experience a powerful example of a leader who was committed to helping him be the best version of himself and placed tremendous trust in him. After graduating from college, thanks to the never-give-up spirit instilled in him by his mother, Garry was able to quickly rise above his peers in the sales roles he took on, which started with door-to-door sales to businesses.

On one occasion, early in his career, Garry carried two bags of product to the door of a store managed by a potential client, who immediately told Garry that he could "Get the f--- out of here." (To eliminate any chance of confusion regarding possible language differences, "Get the f--- out of here" does not mean "Hello" in Australian.)

Garry responded by putting his bags down and sitting on them. The manager of the store said, "What do you think you are doing?"

Garry replied, "You think that I carried these two bags all the way here and you're going to tell me to get out? I'm not leaving here until you at least look at what I have in these cases."

The manager told Garry that he could sit there all night if he wanted to. When the manager came back an hour later, he found Garry still sitting on his bags, apparently willing to sit there all night. He told Garry to go get some beer.

Garry replied, "No problem."

Garry returned with a case of beer, opened a couple, and the two started talking. Two hours later, Garry secured the biggest order his company had ever taken in that area.

Not long after, Garry started working for a company that licensed WD-40 Multi-Use Product. Thanks in large part to his tenacity and deep sense of care for other people, he was promoted often. In 1987, he joined the WD-40 Company as the managing director for Australia. Ten years later, Garry Ridge was named CEO of the company.

At first, he led mostly by leaning on the skills that made him successful as a salesperson. But it didn't take Garry long to realize that the deep care he feels for others would be the most important factor in his success. He gradually shifted his focus more and more to finding ways to bring out the best in others, and eventually wrote a book describing his approach called *Helping People Win at Work*, which he coauthored with Ken Blanchard.

Today, many experts consider Garry Ridge to be one of the most successful business leaders in the world by any measure you use for leadership effectiveness. During his time as the CEO of the WD-40 Company, the company's sales quadrupled, its international sales skyrocketed, and its market capitalization increased from $250 million to $2.5 *billion*.

Garry's mother must be very proud.

While achieving the incredible financial results above, Garry also made a tremendous positive impact on the lives of the employees at the WD-40 Company—who are highly engaged and very happy. Surveys routinely suggest that over 90 percent of WD-40 employees are engaged at work, and nearly 99 percent routinely state, "I love to tell people that I work for the WD-40 Company."

Garry's father must be very proud, too.

Employee Engagement Is a Leadership Thing

Whether conscious or unconscious, the common beliefs about the responsibilities of operations leaders versus the responsibilities of HR / people ops teams seem to be as follows:

1. Operations leaders create strategic goals and plans and manage the execution of those plans. In other words, they "tell people what to do."
2. HR / people ops leaders make sure the workplace culture facilitates employee engagement.

This is the root cause of why the average levels of employee engagement haven't improved in the last twenty years. This is what leads to focusing on the wrong variables for driving employee engagement and not effectively developing great leaders.

The first step to creating and sustaining high levels of engagement is to help leaders realize that employee engagement should be their top priority, tied with strategy for senior leaders in charge of strategy.

It's important to note that a team or organization could have a great strategy or be great at marketing, but still fail. Garry Ridge is regarded as an excellent salesperson, marketer, and strategic thinker. So, one might be tempted to think that the success of the WD-40 Company under his leadership had more to do with marketing, or other strategies, than anything else.

But when I asked Garry about this, he immediately ruled out strategy as the explanation for his success. He said, "The strategy for growth had already been in place for years when I became CEO. What we lacked was a culture that could support high levels of growth."

Garry knew that the best strategy in the world is useless if the people in the organization aren't empowered to effectively execute it. He knew that his top priority was to create and sustain high levels of employee engagement and create processes that help all other leaders to do the same.

For leaders to make employee engagement their top priority, an important shift in mindset is required. Leaders need to operate from the wisdom of what their primary job is.

The primary job of a leader is simply this: *to inspire greatness in one's team.*

Consistently operating from this wisdom is what made Garry Ridge one of the best all-time CEOs in the world. And he's not alone.

In a groundbreaking study conducted by Harvard researchers J. P. Kotter and J. L. Heskett, they tracked 207 publicly traded companies over a period of eleven years. They compared companies that made it a top priority to take good care of employees and bring out the best in them versus companies that were almost entirely focused on profit.

The people-focused companies outperformed their profit-focused competitors by a huge margin. Over eleven years, on average, the people-focused companies increased their net income by 756 percent. The profit-focused companies increased their net income by only 1 percent. This translated into a 901 percent increase in stock price for the people-focused companies versus only a 74 percent increase for the profit-focused companies.

I have yet to meet a person that disagrees with the statement that "the primary job of a leader is to inspire greatness in one's team." In fact, after reading this, you might have thought this statement to be so obvious that it approaches the point of sounding trite.

Interestingly, however, if you were to ask a hundred people what the primary job of a leader is, you would likely get about ninety different answers, and only a few of them might be "inspire greatness" or something very close to that. This lack of clarity around articulating the primary job of a leader results in a lack of clarity about how to be effective as a leader. As a consequence, new managers often don't think of their job as "inspiring greatness," and seasoned leaders, on average, are apparently failing to consistently operate from the wisdom that their primary job is, in fact, to inspire greatness in their teams.

Most new managers are promoted because they're really good at their jobs. When they become a manager, they continue doing what they've always done to be successful: they work hard on individual-contributor-type tasks, while trying to squeeze in leadership behaviors, which often amount to little more than telling people what to do.

Unfortunately, these high performers often fail as leaders because they either don't know that their primary job is now to inspire greatness in their team members, or they haven't been trained how to do it, or both. They often incorrectly think that leadership behaviors are about "managing people."

Seasoned managers usually know that their primary job is inspiring greatness in their team members. But they either rarely find the time to do it because they're caught up in dealing with urgent issues, they haven't developed habits and routines for consistently behaving in ways that inspire greatness, and/or they've never been trained how to consistently bring out the best in their team members.

Anyone Can Inspire Greatness, If They Have the Right Motivation

Although "inspiring greatness" might sound like some lofty aspiration that only "natural-born leaders" (often thought to be people with high levels of charisma) could ever attain, it's actually quite simple to do.

It's not easy, but it is simple. There is a process to it, which you'll learn in the pages that follow.

This means that anyone fit to be promoted to a management position—whether or not one is a "natural born" or charismatic leader—can inspire greatness in others.

To inspire greatness in their teams, leaders must serve as coaches who are obsessed with helping others to thrive: to be happy, great human beings, who do great work. They must work continuously to create the conditions for such greatness and help identify and remove obstacles to greatness for the individuals on their teams. Leaders must also create the conditions for, and remove the obstacles to, team members being able to consistently work together as effectively as possible.

However, the motivation for these efforts is *extremely important*. Every leader wants her team members to do great work, and for her team to get great results. But if the motivation is selfish, the leader is almost certain to fail.

Selfish leaders often demand high levels of performance because they want to look good, get a promotion, or get a raise. They tend to think in terms of *How can I get more out of my people?*

But this motivation has a palpable energy associated with it. We can feel it when people have selfish motivations, and it's repulsive. Selfish leaders eventually repel talented people of high character.

Great leaders want team members to be happy, great human beings who do great work not to benefit the leader, but because that's what's best for the team members. When people consistently do great work and positively impact others along the way, they feel good about themselves and truly enjoy their work. This results in greater happiness and satisfaction in life.

Great leaders tend to think in terms of *How can I give my team members what they need to thrive?* Just as with the selfish motivation, there is a palpable energy that accompanies this pure, selfless motivation that arises when a leader has the best interests of the team member in mind. Employees at the WD-40 Company could "feel" that the top priority of Garry Ridge and other leaders in the company was to help people be the best version of themselves.

And this energy, which is an essential element of inspiring greatness, is very attractive. People want to work with leaders like this, and they are extremely likely to go the extra mile for leaders like this.

Great leaders don't *demand* performance. They *inspire* it.

Why Leaders Don't See Most Opportunities for Inspiring Greatness

I would guess that you, like most people, have experienced some variation of the following scenario:

You purchase a new product, like a car. Prior to you owning this new car, you never really noticed this particular model while you were going about your day. But after you purchased the new car, you started seeing it everywhere. It seemed like your car suddenly became the most popular model on the road.

There are several possible explanations for why this phenomenon occurred.

It's certainly possible that you are very cool, and when other people found out that you bought this car they all went out and bought it, too. However, I think there is solid evidence to suggest that there is another, more likely explanation.

There are areas of the brain that are responsible for filtering out from conscious awareness any information that is not important, which is almost all of the information the brain receives. Many neuroscientists believe that the reticular formation, or reticular activating system, is at least partially responsible for this work.

It is estimated that the human nervous system can process eleven million bits of information every second. Research suggests that, thanks to the areas of the brain responsible for filtering out most information, less than one hundred bits of information arise in conscious awareness each second.

This means that we are blind to roughly 99.9991 percent of the information received by the nervous system. We only consciously see 0.0009 percent of that information.

Thus, I believe that the more likely explanation for why the new car seemed to appear everywhere after you bought it is that it had actually already been everywhere before you bought it. However, your subconscious mind did not include this car in the "important information" category. As a result, even though the car was almost certainly just as popular before you bought it as it appeared to be after you bought it, your brain kept you from seeing it.

Once you bought the car, it was moved into the "important information" category in your brain, so areas of the brain like the reticular formation started allowing that information to be processed in conscious awareness. In other words, your brain allowed you to see the car that it had previously kept you from seeing.

Filtering out unimportant information serves an important purpose. If we had to consciously process even a fraction of the eleven million bits of information that we receive each second, we would probably lose our minds. Some researchers believe that conditions like attention deficit disorder and schizophrenia may be the result of allowing just a tiny percentage more of unimportant information into conscious awareness than most brains allow.

Although areas of the brain like the reticular formation are likely essential for preventing us from going insane due to information overload, there are some important ramifications. Unfortunately, most of us in Western society have likely been the subject of extensive conditioning that has resulted in the subconscious mind having several suboptimal ideas about what is most important for leaders to be effective.

This conditioning causes us to think that traditionally macho traits— like winning or hitting the numbers—are most important, especially in sports and business. This conditioning can prevent us from seeing the information that is most important for creating the conditions for consistently high levels of performance. It can literally blind us to critical leadership abilities, like the ability to see opportunities to help team members to be happy, great human beings who do great work, to see obstacles getting in the way of such greatness, or to see opportunities for us to grow our abilities to inspire greatness in our teams.

In order for leaders to have any chance of being able to consistently bring out the best in our teams, we must undo the conditioning that prevents us from behaving as though inspiring greatness is our top priority. That's why the first step in the four-step process you'll learn in this book involves undoing harmful conditioning.

Step 1: Clarify and Continuously Remind Ourselves and Other Leaders That the Primary Job of a Leader Is to Inspire Greatness in Others

A simple yet powerful hack for undoing the conditioning that blinds you to opportunities to inspire greatness is to simply rewrite your job description. This doesn't mean going to HR and formally requesting a new job description.

All you need to do is print up your current job description and write at the top of it, "Additional Responsibilities." Then, write out and print on a separate piece of paper, in big, bold font, your primary job as a leader, which should be something like the following:

My primary job is to inspire greatness in my team by serving as a coach who consistently helps people to be happy, great human beings, who do great work.

Once you have written out your new job description, it is important that you review it several times a day for the next thirty days. This simple practice can help you rewire your brain and undo the conditioning that has programmed your brain to be blind to the most important information required for leadership excellence.

Even if you think you already know that your primary job is to inspire greatness, and that you're doing fairly well at it, I highly recommend you engage in this practice. Toward the end of my first meeting with Garry Ridge, he pulled out a notebook with some bullet points on the front. The bullet points are all reminders of who he wants to be as a person and as a leader.

Even after decades of realizing extraordinary success as a leader, Garry carries this notebook everywhere he goes and reviews the bullet points multiple times every day. The bullet points can be summarized as follows: "My primary job is to inspire greatness in others."

To give you an idea of how important this practice is, I have actually heard very well-intentioned leaders who consciously believe that their primary job is to inspire greatness in their teams say things like the following:

"I have to take time away from my job to spend time coaching my team members."

I cringe when I hear things like that. If you're a leader, coaching team members to be happy, great human beings, who do great work, *is your job*. The difference in language may seem subtle, but it tells us a lot about what leaders subconsciously think the primary job of a leader is. They subconsciously believe—and often behave as though—the primary job of a leader is whatever is in their job description.

And I have never seen a leader's job description start with "My primary job is to inspire greatness in my team by serving as a coach who consistently helps people be happy, great human beings and do great work," unless it was someone who followed my advice to do so.

Just to be clear, we're not talking about "The Secret" here, which is commonly interpreted to be some variation of "If you think about something often enough it will become real." However, by reciting your new job description multiple times a day for a while, your mind will be a little more open to opportunities to inspire greatness, and you'll spend a little more time thinking about and behaving in ways that help you focus more on inspiring greatness in your team. Thus, reciting your new job description will work in tandem with new thoughts and actions to gradually change your subconscious beliefs so you spend more time operating from the wisdom that your primary job as a leader is to inspire greatness.

This shift is the first and foundational step of the simple yet extremely effective four-step process for improving leadership effectiveness outlined in this book, which can be applied by any leader to consistently inspire greatness in others, whether or not they're a "natural born" or highly charismatic leader.

The Shift That Changes Everything

When leaders can make the shift to consistently operating from the wisdom that their primary job is to inspire greatness in their teams, an elegant solution naturally unfolds for creating high levels of employee engagement. This solution resolves all three of the issues, outlined in chapter one, that have resulted in the average levels of employee engagement not improving in the last twenty years.

Clearly, *inspiring greatness* is synonymous with *inspiring engagement*. Engaged employees are the ones who go the extra mile to accomplish the mission. When leaders realize that their primary job is to inspire greatness, it changes the entire approach to employee engagement.

It is no longer seen as a project that is the responsibility of HR. Instead, employee engagement is seen as the top priority for every leader in the organization. Leaders at all levels shift attention to the most important work there is for them: inspiring greatness in their teams.

Of course, the question that arises for many at this point is, *How do I consistently inspire greatness in my team?*

The rest of this book is devoted to the next three steps of the simple process—supported by decades of research—to consistently inspire greatness in others and help leaders at all levels dramatically improve their abilities to sustain high levels of employee engagement and performance.

The next three steps in the process flow naturally and logically from the key first principle that the primary job of a leader is to inspire greatness in one's team.

• • • Action Items for Chapter 2 • • •

1. Please print up your current job description and write at the top of it, "Additional Responsibilities."

2. Please write out and print on a separate piece of paper, in big, bold font, your primary job as a leader, which should be something like the following:

> My primary job is to inspire greatness in my team by serv-
> ing as a coach who consistently helps people to be happy,
> great human beings who do great work.

3. Please go create three 5-minute events with pop-up reminders on your calendar that repeat every morning, midday, and afternoon for the next thirty days that remind you to read out loud your new job description and take five minutes to think of at least one action you could take to help team members to be happier, better human beings who do great work.

3

How to Know Whether You're Helping People to Be Great, or Getting in Their Way

Parents often hear about a stage of childhood development referred to as the "terrible twos." This is a time when emotions develop rapidly for children, but they have little or no ability to regulate them.

My wife and I were pleasantly surprised when our son turned three and we had yet to deal with any of the serious meltdowns that are often associated with the terrible twos. We naively thought maybe we would just never deal with those things because our son was "so advanced, emotionally."

Little did we know that the terrible twos often don't really begin until the child turns three and can sometimes peak when a child is four. Our celebration of making it successfully through age two abruptly ended shortly after our son's third birthday.

His third year of life was challenging, at best, much of the time. On the bright side, my wife and I developed a lot of patience and applied a lot of time and energy navigating the emotional roller coaster that seemed to define much of our three-year-old's life. This helped us develop valuable skills for all areas of our lives.

We were really hoping that because the third year was so challenging, we would see significant improvement during his fourth year. As it turned out, not so much.

I remember one particularly notable day shortly after my son turned four. He was building a structure with one of our favorite toys, called Magna-Tiles®. Magna-Tiles are amazing for allowing children to build complex, three-dimensional structures, and I highly recommend them to any parent. However, the structures built with Magna-Tiles are somewhat fragile and can easily be knocked down with even the most gentle of accidental collisions.

My son asked me to watch him simulate an airplane flight as he moved across the room, so I slid back just a little bit to give him some space. When I did, I accidentally bumped into a structure he had built with the Magna-Tiles.

As soon as he heard and saw the structure being damaged, he started screaming, tears quickly filled his eyes, and he wound up—in what seemed like almost comical slow-motion—to punch me in the arm. He had never hit anyone up to that point in his life and, judging by his technique, I'm guessing he learned how to do this by seeing a child younger than him hitting somebody else on the playground at school.

The look on his face after he hit me in the arm was priceless. It was a mix of frustration, sadness, and confusion. He looked as though he wasn't sure how his hand moved in my direction and collided with my arm.

Although I certainly don't claim to be perfect at this, in this instance I was able to remain calm and apply one of the most powerful habits I have developed over the years. As I assessed the situation, I took a moment to think about what my son might need.

I knew that he had been a little whiny the entire afternoon, so I suspected that in addition to being in a developmental stage where emotions are challenging, he was also probably a little hungry and tired. This, of course, is a bad combination for anybody, especially a four-year-old who is just starting to deal with powerful emotions.

I knew that I would need to address the importance of not using violence to solve problems soon, but I also knew that discussion would be more constructive after I helped my son navigate the emotional turbulence.

So the first thing I did was ask him, "Are you feeling frustrated because I knocked down the structure you built?"

He started crying again and loudly said, "Yeah!"

Although asking a child to become aware of the emotion they feel often seems to temporarily exacerbate the situation, it's a crucial first step for helping them develop the ability to effectively deal with their emotions.

I then asked, "What do you think you need right now?"

He looked at me, with tears running off his face, and simply said, "I need a hug."

I gave him a hug and we snuggled for a few minutes as he calmed down. Once he was calm again, I gave him a little extra snack (something I knew he needed), and we talked about different ways to respond to feeling frustrated that don't involve screaming or hitting people.

I'll never forget the look he gave me right before he went back to playing. Without saying a word, his expression said it all: *You understand me. You really care. I feel much better as a result.*

The rest of the afternoon was free of meltdowns and instead filled with laughter and fun.

Although I would never suggest that employees are like children, in many ways being an effective leader is like being an effective parent. I believe that a simple definition of successful parenting is raising a child who is happy, treats others with kindness and respect, and makes a positive contribution to our society.

In other words, a successful parent is one who inspires greatness in her children.

For leaders, much like for parents, the real work is creating the conditions for greatness by identifying and meeting the most important needs people have for being happy, great human beings and doing great work, and helping to remove obstacles to such greatness. Put another way, our job as leaders is to identify and meet the most important needs people have for thriving, both professionally and personally, and help remove obstacles to thriving.

Step 2: Identify the Needs People Have for Thriving at Work

When leaders spend more time operating from the wisdom that their true job is to inspire greatness in their teams, it logically follows that the next action they need to take is to identify the most important needs people have for thriving (being happy, great human beings who do great work).

There are two categories of needs that people have for thriving at work. There are universal needs, which apply to almost everyone in almost every type of organization. And there are unique needs, which could be unique to your organization or to an individual on your team. You'll learn more about uncovering unique needs in several chapters in Part 2.

I strongly recommend initially focusing your efforts on identifying and meeting the universal needs that people have for thriving at work. There are two reasons for this.

First, there is no work required for you to identify the universal needs. They are well known, so you don't need to go figure this out on your own. There are fourteen of these needs for thriving at work, listed below, which decades of research suggest are most strongly correlated with employee engagement and retention.

Second, as you, and any leaders who report to you, continue to grow in your ability to meet these universal needs, and continue to rewire your brain to see inspiring greatness as your primary job, you will naturally improve at your ability to identify and meet the unique needs.

Universal Needs for Thriving at Work

Following are the fourteen universal needs people have for thriving at work (for being great, happy human beings, who do great work), and for being engaged at work. There is an abundance of research, collected over decades, demonstrating that in organizations with leaders who consistently meet the following fourteen universal needs, employee engagement is very high. In organizations with leaders who fail to consistently meet these needs, engagement is low.

1. **Appreciation/Recognition:** People need to feel recognized and/or appreciated so they know they are making a contribution.
2. **Autonomy:** People need to feel that they have as much control as possible over their lives.
3. **Belonging:** People need to feel that they are part of a group with mutual respect and care, and shared values.
4. **Clarity of Expectations:** A lack of clarity is a significant source of anxiety and frustration.
5. **Doing Work That Leverages Strengths:** The more time people spend doing work they enjoy and are good at, the more likely they are to be engaged.
6. **Excellence:** People inherently want and need to do a great job.
7. **Feedback:** People need regular, helpful feedback.
8. **Feeling Like One's Opinion Matters / Is Heard:** People need to feel like their ideas matter.
9. **Feeling Cared For by One's Manager:** This is the most powerful driver of engagement, and the foundation for meeting all other needs. People need to know that their manager cares about them as a person and works to help them be a happy, great human being who does great work.
10. **Growth:** People need to be continuously growing.
11. **Having the Tools Required to Do One's Job:** Lacking the tools to do one's job is a significant source of anxiety and frustration.

12. **Meaningful Work:** People need to find meaning at work.
13. **Trust:** People need to know that they can trust their coworkers, most importantly their leaders.
14. **Well-Being:** People need to be able to go to work without adverse effects on their physical and emotional well-being.

Step 3: Get Feedback on How Well Direct Managers Are Meeting Needs

Thich Nhat Hanh (pronounced "Tick Knot Hahn") could have lived the type of life that most monks lived in his tradition, mainly cloistered in a monastery. He was, in fact, often encouraged to do so. But he knew that just outside the monastery, his brothers and sisters in Vietnam were experiencing tremendous suffering as the result of the raging war there.

He decided that he needed to find a balance of time in the monastery and time spent actively relieving the suffering of his brothers and sisters, as well as the American service members who were stationed there trying to defend the central and southern parts of the country from the attackers from the north. Thay (as he was affectionately known by his students) did not just immediately begin working to solve problems, however obvious some of them might have appeared. He knew that to be of most help to others he first needed to understand their pain.

Thay spent most of his time simply being with people, listening to their pain. This enabled him to build tremendous levels of trust with others, and to act in ways that would be most helpful and best leverage his efforts. His work caught the attention of many in the West, who were very impressed with his approach. He was eventually nominated for the Nobel Peace Prize by Martin Luther King Jr.

After the war ended, Thay continued to work to relieve the suffering of others, focusing much of his energy on helping families thrive. One of the practices he taught, which I engage in regularly and highly recommend, is to periodically sit down with the people you love and hold their hand. After a moment or so of sitting and being with your loved one, look them in the eyes and ask the simple question, "How can I love you better?"

Making this a habit in your personal life can help you develop a similar habit as a leader, and vice versa. The skill is highly transferable. Although in a work situation you might not ask the question using those exact words, the intention behind the approach is the same.

This practice can positively and dramatically transform relationships in a way that is essential for inspiring greatness in team members. And if a leader, or leadership team, is truly committed to inspiring greatness in team members, some variation of this practice is the next logical step after identifying the needs people have for thriving.

We need to get regular feedback from team members on how well we, and other direct managers, are meeting the needs people have for thriving, asking some variation of the question "How can I better help you to thrive?"

The feedback we get is absolutely essential for helping us improve our ability to effectively lead our teams. We all have blind spots. Most of us have a lot of them.

Research from Dr. Tasha Eurich, author of the excellent book on self-awareness *Insight*, showed that while 95 percent of people think that they are moderately or highly self-aware, less than 15 percent of people actually are. If leaders don't get regular feedback from team members on how well they're doing, the chances of being successful are slim to none.

Unfortunately, most direct reports are at least somewhat uncomfortable providing constructive feedback to the boss. Even when there is a good relationship between manager and direct report, it's hard to get the best feedback unless we allow feedback to be delivered anonymously.

This is why most organizations use some type of third-party software tool to collect feedback. (If you're part of a small team or organization, you could create your own surveys using something as simple as Google Forms.) However, most organizations make some fatal mistakes with their approach to getting the feedback that is essential for consistently inspiring greatness in team members.

Many organizations try to get feedback with large annual employee engagement surveys. Unfortunately, this approach of trying to identify with one large survey all of the issues that are negatively affecting employee engagement almost never works. In fact, it often does more harm than good.

There are three principal reasons large surveys fail:

1. Too Much Information

First, the leadership team usually ends up with a large number of issues they need to fix to improve employee engagement and retention. Often, in the worst-case scenario, the leadership team is so overwhelmed with the work they need to do to fix the issues that they do nothing at all.

Of course, if the organization does nothing at all, they would have been better off not even doing a survey. If we ask employees for their feedback using a survey, there is an expectation that something will be done to address the feedback.

Failing to act on surveys tends to further reduce employee engagement. Employees feel like it was a waste of their time to take the survey (which can take as long as thirty minutes), they feel like no one in management really listens to them, and they trust management even less than they did before the survey.

2. Focused on the Wrong Variables

The second reason typical employee engagement surveys fail—or make things worse—is that they often focus on variables that have very little impact on employee engagement. These surveys focus on organization-wide issues that seem best addressed with perks or big policy changes. Instead, employee engagement surveys should be heavily focused on behaviors of direct managers because they are the primary drivers of employee engagement.

As you learned in chapter one, research from Gallup has shown that at least 70 percent of employee engagement is driven by employees' direct managers. So, any strategy for improving employee engagement must focus heavily on leaders at all levels.

3. Questions That Don't Lead to Action

The third reason typical employee engagement surveys fail is that, unfortunately, even when they do include questions about leaders, they usually fail to link results to simple, actionable behaviors. For example, many companies do an annual survey asking how confident employees feel about the CEO, core leadership, and their manager. The answer to this question doesn't provide any direction for action. A dissatisfactory answer to this could mean an employee doesn't feel appreciated, or it could mean they don't agree with some recent decisions.

Asking questions like this results in a tremendous amount of work—which is usually delegated to the HR team and sucks up dozens or hundreds of work hours—to figure out how to translate the results into an action plan that will help managers make a better impact on employee engagement. It often takes so long to do this that employees don't associate changes they see with the feedback they provide. Thus, even when something positive does happen, there's still the perception that nothing was done in response to employee feedback, which results in a loss of confidence and trust in the leadership team that can negate any positive changes in the behaviors of leaders.

A Better Way to Get the Feedback We Need

To see improvements in employee engagement and retention quickly and sustainably, I strongly recommend that you start by creating a strong foundation of regular feedback that creates a virtuous cycle, as pictured below, in which employees regularly give feedback, feel heard, and see action being taken on their feedback within a few days.

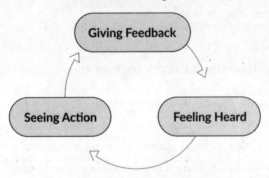

In order to accomplish this, you should do very short, focused, anonymous surveys every couple of weeks. Each survey should consist of one or two questions on how well direct managers are meeting just one universal need of their team members.

It is only after establishing the foundation of this virtuous cycle by using short surveys focused on behaviors of direct managers for at least six months that I would recommend doing a survey on organization-wide issues or any type of open-ended, exploratory survey. To get a general measure of employee engagement, I recommend a short, "pulse" survey of just three to five questions focusing on needs like well-being (happiness), meaning, growth, excellence, and how well managers care for team members.

In the Appendix, you'll find a detailed, helpful guide to using various types of surveys in the most effective ways to uncover unknown issues and get the data you need to measure progress while ensuring that your measurement efforts don't have a negative impact on employee engagement, as they very often do. Also, if your organization is committed to doing a large annual survey soon (or just did one), or if you're committed to them for the purposes of qualifying for awards,

you'll find helpful guidance in the Appendix for applying the system outlined in
this chapter in combination with the large annual surveys.

There are multiple reasons why this approach of using short, frequent surveys focused on the behaviors of direct managers is so effective.

First, and most important, as you learned in chapter one, more than 70 percent of employee engagement and retention is driven by behaviors of the employees' direct managers. By focusing on direct managers, you can make the biggest impact in the least amount of time. This is the most highly leveraged approach.

Research from Gallup makes it clear that the organizations with the highest levels of employee engagement and retention are the ones with the most engaged managers who consistently meet the fourteen universal needs people have for thriving and being engaged at work. And having engaged managers is not only good for your organization's performance, it's good for the managers.

The easier we can make it for managers to consistently meet the legitimate needs of employees, the more meaning they'll find in their work. This means that work becomes less stressful and more fulfilling. As an added bonus, engaged managers are less likely to leave, which will help you reduce turnover among managers. Research published by Shawn Achor and his colleagues in the *Harvard Business Review* found that the average person would give up roughly 25 percent of their lifetime earnings to consistently do meaningful work.

Second, it only takes about sixty seconds for employees to complete a short survey with one to three questions on it, so they don't find the surveys annoying or disruptive.

Third, by getting regular feedback in small bits, it's easier for managers to digest and act on that feedback. Managers don't have to think about a large number of issues at once. They just have to work on growing in one small area, so they're much more likely to take action.

Finally, it's possible to increase employee engagement just by asking the survey questions in the right context. Instead of being framed as part of an "employee engagement" survey, which many employees feel is about finding ways to get more work out of them, I recommend the context be about managers doing a better job at helping people to thrive. This approach comes naturally to leaders who consistently operate from the wisdom of knowing that their primary job is to inspire greatness in team members by serving as a coach who helps team members to be happy, great human beings who do great work.

When you ask questions in the context of "How can I help you thrive?" you're sending the message that you actually care about team members as people, which research from Gallup and others suggests is the most powerful driver of employee engagement. By quickly taking meaningful action on the feedback you receive, even if it's not perfect action, you further strengthen the perception team members have that you truly care about them.

• • • Action Items for Chapter 3 • • •

1. Please create a document that lists the fourteen universal needs people have for thriving at work, print it, and keep it near your new job description. You could copy and paste these from a blog article I wrote for *Business Leadership Today*.

   Here's the web address: https://businessleadershiptoday.com /how-to-improve-employee-engagement/.

2. Please write out a plan for how you'll get feedback on behaviors that address the fourteen universal needs people have for thriving at work (Part 2 will provide many of these behaviors for you).

4

Leadership Development That Creates a Lasting Impact and Facilitates an Almost Instant Response to Employee Feedback

From 2004 to 2006, not long after graduating from Lehigh University with a degree in mechanical engineering, Mark Roberge attended Massachusetts Institute of Technology (MIT). Rather than working on an advanced degree in engineering, though, he was part of the Masters of Business Administration (MBA) program at the MIT Sloan School of Management.

In one of his entrepreneurship classes, he participated in a business idea competition. Out of fifty ideas that were presented, students in the class could vote for three. The twelve students whose ideas received the most votes were then named as CEOs. Those CEOs then got to present a three-minute "elevator pitch" in front of the class, and the rest of the students got to decide which CEOs they wanted to work with. Once the teams were finalized, they began working to transform their business ideas into real businesses outside the classroom.

Mark's business idea, a social site for pet owners, was one of the twelve that ended up with the most votes. Another student who made the cut was Dharmesh Shah. His idea was a company that helped businesses leverage inbound marketing.

Dharmesh and Mark ended up becoming friends. Mark was very excited about Dharmesh's business, so Dharmesh asked Mark to help out one or two days per week.

Soon, Mark was selling for Dharmesh's growing company, and was landing about as many sales as one of the cofounders of the company. After the founders learned they were going to receive venture capital, they offered Mark a full-time position as the senior vice president (SVP) of sales and services. Since Mark's social site was not going as well as he would have liked, he decided to take the position at Dharmesh's company, called HubSpot.

Seven years later, Mark had grown his sales and services team at HubSpot to 425 employees, his team had acquired over 10,000 customers, annual sales exceeded $100 million, HubSpot achieved a $1 billion valuation after its initial public offering (IPO), and Mark became the bestselling author of *The Sales Acceleration Formula*.

One of the misconceptions about sales is that introverted people, which engineers tend to be, don't make good salespeople. There are many traits common among engineers that actually make them great salespeople. And, apparently, engineering traits can also help people be successful SVPs of sales.

One of the keys to Mark's success was applying an engineering approach to sales systems. He relied heavily on data to help inform all decisions, including hiring. After some early failures in hiring, Mark decided to do a regression analysis to determine which traits of salespeople were most predictive of success.

Much to his surprise, coachability turned out to be the most powerful predictor of successful salespeople at HubSpot. Armed with this information, Mark and his team tweaked their interview process to test for coachability and worked to hire the most coachable people.

Realizing how important coaching was for success, Mark also looked deeply into the question of how to best coach people, and discovered that most people aren't naturally good at coaching. What he often saw was sales managers sitting down with sales reps and essentially vomiting information for twenty minutes at a time. Sales reps would be overwhelmed and few of the ideas, if any, would stick. Not surprisingly, this "vomit" approach proved to be very ineffective.

Mark realized that sales is one of the few areas in an organization where it's possible to have objective measures of almost every step of the process. Of course, we know which people hit their sales quota. But we can also easily track things like how many calls people make, which opening lines are most effective for a given audience, how many initial calls turn into demo appointments, and how many demo calls convert to sales.

What the effective coaches on Mark's team were able to do was zero in on which step in the process sales reps were struggling with the most. Then, instead of vomiting ten ideas in twenty minutes, they would offer brief guidance on a couple of ways to improve and ask the sales rep to practice with one of the new behaviors for a while to see how it worked.

This subtle shift in approach to coaching and training was game changing for Mark's team, and can be game changing for anyone who coaches or trains others. Several months before learning about Mark Roberge, I had a similar insight as it relates to leadership training. This insight forms the foundation for solving the problems that have resulted in the average levels of employee engagement not improving in the last twenty years.

I realized that just as collecting feedback in large chunks is ineffective and often does more harm than good, delivering leadership training in large chunks is also very ineffective, just as it was with sales coaching on Mark's teams at HubSpot. The following example helps to illustrate why.

Imagine a person named Amy is trying to learn how to shoot free throws in basketball, and she works with two different coaches. The first coach she works with watches her shoot a couple of balls, but doesn't have the expertise to know what changes will provide the biggest impact, and doesn't have much coaching experience.

This first coach takes ten minutes to talk, and he gives Amy ten suggestions during that time, much like many of the sales managers Mark Roberge observed in the early years of HubSpot.

The suggestions include things like, "You need more knee bend. Your elbow needs to be under your hand. Your feet need to be pointed at the goal." And so on.

Working with this first coach, how much do you think Amy is going to improve?

The second coach Amy works with has the expertise to know what change is going to make the biggest impact. So, she says to Amy in a few seconds, "Your elbow needs to be under your hand. Please try keeping your elbow under your hand and take fifty shots like that."

Thanks to the second coach, Amy sees results quickly, which motivates her. And, by focusing on that one, highly leveraged change before she starts working on the next change, it's much more likely that the first change will stick.

The approach of the first coach is very information heavy, and light on implementation, much like the approach utilized in most leadership training programs. This is one of the primary reasons leadership training so often fails to make any lasting impact.

Leadership training is often conducted as a finite "project," much like typical employee engagement surveys. Training tends to be conducted once or twice a year, and participants attend long sessions ranging from a half day to multiple days. These training sessions tend to be very focused on delivering information.

After attending these long training sessions, leaders do often walk away with lots of great ideas that they really want to implement. Unfortunately, when these leaders get back to the office on Monday and reality "punches them in the face," they get caught up with what seems urgent, and they usually apply little to nothing of what they learned. What they do apply often doesn't stick because when leadership development is viewed as a finite "project," there isn't a follow-up plan for helping leaders transform the new behaviors into lasting habits.

This is a pain I'm intimately familiar with. There have been many occasions when I finished delivering a leadership training program and everyone was very inspired and energized. They had proven, actionable ideas to go implement, and accountability partners to help turn ideas into action.

I would leave the event feeling energized by all the positive comments attendees had shared with me during and after the training program. Then I would get on the airplane to go home, and cry. I knew that because the organization wasn't willing to invest in a follow-up system to transform information into action, very little change was going to occur.

This is not to say that in-person training is not useful. It certainly can be. It can provide the big picture and context for the follow-up program, and ensure that people begin said program inspired to grow and make an impact. However, to produce measurable, *lasting* change, there *must be* a follow-up system to transform information into new behaviors that are repeated, and thus become new habits that stick.

For some reason, many people seem to believe that big changes can happen quickly. But they almost never do.

Imagine a friend said to you, "My body fat is currently twenty percent and I bench two hundred pounds. I'd like to get my body fat down to ten percent and bench three twenty-five. My plan for hitting these goals is to go to the gym for forty-eight hours straight and work out as hard as I can!"

You would probably look at your friend as though he is crazy. But if your friend said he planned to hit his goals by going to the gym for twenty minutes a day, four days per week, for a year, you would think his plan was very realistic.

Likewise, we often seem to think that reading one book (even this one), or attending one training program, is going to make us great leaders. It won't. However, if we develop a small new habit for inspiring greatness in our teams every two weeks over the course of a year, we could realize incredible improvements in our leadership effectiveness.

The approach to leadership development you'll learn in this chapter makes this possible and solves several of the key problems that have resulted in most leadership training making no lasting impact.

Context Matters

First, by including leadership development as part of the four-step process presented in this book, you help provide a context for all leadership training that inspires people to take action on what they learn.

When leadership training is offered outside of a holistic system for improving engagement and performance, attendees often don't go into the training with an eagerness to learn. They often don't see how a workshop on listening skills, for instance, fits into the big picture, or into goals that are important to them. But when training is offered in the context of a holistic system for *inspiring greatness in their team members*, it's easy to connect training topics to the big picture.

And, by linking training to the big picture of inspiring greatness by serving as a coach who helps team members to thrive, we tap into a powerful aspiration that lies within all of us: the aspiration to make a difference in the lives of others. By focusing training on behaviors that help meet the needs people have for thriving, every training can easily be aligned with this very logical and inspiring context of inspiring greatness in others.

This also helps provide the constant reminders needed to undo the conditioning you learned about in chapter two, and more consistently operate from the wisdom that the primary job of leaders is to inspire greatness in others.

Step 4: A Simple Hack for Almost Instantly Acting on Feedback

In addition to providing inspiring context for training, the four-step process you're learning in this book helps you close the time gap between feedback and training, which may be the most powerful element of this approach. Employee feedback and leadership training need to be synchronized as tightly as possible to see significant, consistent improvements in employee motivation and engagement. There are two keys to making this happen.

First, for at least the first six months, you should only ask questions on your surveys that address issues you know you *should* address, and that you know you *can* address.

You know that you should address how well managers are meeting the universal needs their direct reports have for thriving at work. Decades of research makes it clear that meeting these needs is the most highly leveraged activity leaders can engage in for inspiring high levels of employee engagement. And, because these needs are public knowledge, you know you *can* address them, either with training or, if you're part of a small team or organization without the resources to create or invest in training, through personal study (which Part 2 will help with).

As a reminder, in the Appendix, you'll find a detailed, helpful guide to using various types of surveys in the most effective ways to uncover unknown issues and get the data you need to measure progress while ensuring that your measurement efforts don't have a negative impact on employee engagement, as they very often do.

Second, by focusing initially on how well managers are meeting the universal needs employees have for thriving at work, you can apply a simple, incredibly powerful hack for acting on employee feedback almost instantly. Instead of sending out surveys and then coming up with a plan after you receive the feedback, all you need to do is have training ready to go on how to consistently meet a need *before* any surveys are deployed.

For instance, if you know you're going to send out a survey on the universal need for feeling appreciated, you should have a brief, five-minute training (ideally live or video) already created before the survey goes out, focused on a simple habit for better showing appreciation, so that managers can watch and take action on the training as soon as they get the feedback from their direct reports.

(If you're part of a small team or organization without the resources to create or invest in training, you should study and have a plan for how you'll better show appreciation before the survey goes out.)

This approach for tightly synchronizing feedback with training is extremely important for several reasons.

1. Linking Training to Feedback Improves Training Effectiveness

First, one explanation for why most leadership training fails to make any lasting impact is that people aren't as open to learning something new if they don't think they're deficient in the area being taught. Imagine a team of leaders is told that they're going to attend a training on listening skills. A large percentage of those leaders (remember, less than 15 percent of people are moderately to highly self-aware) are going to think something like the following:

I'm a great listener. I don't need this training. What a waste of time. I'd rather get stuff done.

You may have smiled or laughed when you read the words above, but I have spoken with learning and development professionals in large companies who have received feedback almost exactly like that from leaders who have attended a training.

For any leader who attends the training with the aforementioned attitude going in, it's unlikely that they are going to be open to the training, much less act on what they learn. However, if leaders had just received feedback from team members letting them know that their listening skills are perceived as a 3.7 out of 6, it's more likely that they'll be open to the training, particularly if they can connect improving in that area to their own goals.

2. Focusing on Habit Formation Is the Secret to Lasting Results

The second reason you should have training ready before the survey goes out, and have it focused on meeting just one need, is that instead of being overwhelmed with lots of different things to work on, managers just have one area to work on. If the training provides just a couple of simple, actionable ideas for improving, it's much more likely that the managers will take some action. And because the managers are only working on one new leadership behavior at a time, they are much more likely to make that new behavior a habit that sticks.

The approach to leadership training I recommend is to apply the insight Mark Roberge and I had about coaching and training, and emulate the example of the second basketball coach mentioned in the example above. This can be done by focusing on the most important behaviors for inspiring employee engagement, and teaching those behaviors in small, digestible bits. Just as it helped Amy quickly improve her free throws, the approach of offering short training on one behavior at a time provides managers lots of time to act on the information they receive, see results, and form a habit that sticks, before learning about a new behavior.

This is the key to helping people create lasting transformation. People very rarely change much as a result of receiving new information, however exciting the new information is. Lasting transformation occurs gradually over time, like the changes you could see after regularly going to the gym for a year.

Lasting transformation can be effectively realized when we are provided simple, easy-to-stick-with behaviors to try and held accountable for trying them. When those behaviors are the ones that make a significant impact, and at least some impact can be seen quickly, it's much more likely that those behaviors will be repeated. When those behaviors are repeated, they soon become habits that we are very likely to stick with. As more and more of these simple micro-habits develop, significant, lasting changes occur.

(On a side note, I read *Atomic Habits* by James Clear after writing this manuscript. If you have not read that book, I highly recommend it for helping to create behavior change.)

3. Seamless Integration Improves Results

The third reason that this approach of timely, focused, short training is so effective is that it doesn't interrupt managers' work with a half day or full day of training, as traditional leadership training does. With the approach recommended here, the manager likely only misses fifteen minutes or so, including the time to read the feedback, watch the training, and take the first steps to creating a new habit for improving. So, when leaders go back to their workflow, they are much less likely to feel overwhelmed with things they fell behind on.

Also, because the manager can consume the training in their working environment, they can immediately act on it while it's still fresh in their minds. They don't need to wait to "get back to the office."

Taking less time out of a manager's workflow, and offering training that can be consumed while managers are in their normal working environment, is another way to significantly increase the chances that the manager will take action on and stick with what she learned in the training.

4. Tightly Synchronizing Training with Feedback in and of Itself Improves Employee Engagement

Finally, and perhaps most important, this approach of tightly synchronizing employee feedback with leadership development, by having quick, focused training ready to go before surveys go out, also helps ensure that employees see action being taken on their feedback in a matter of days.

I recommend that each survey is only open for a couple of days, and that leaders are asked to watch the training within two or three business days of the survey closing. I also recommend that each leader's direct manager hold the leader accountable for taking some action, even if not perfect action, on the feedback and training they receive.

With this approach, instead of the employee engagement feedback process hurting employee engagement, as it usually does, the feedback process in and of itself can actually improve employee engagement. This approach allows you to build a virtuous cycle of employees sharing feedback, feeling heard, and quickly seeing action taken on their feedback.

Virtuous Cycle

With each cycle of this simple process, employees have more confidence and trust in their managers and in the leadership team.

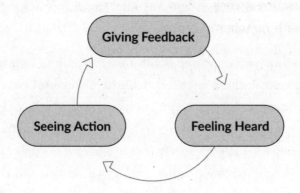

Trust Grows

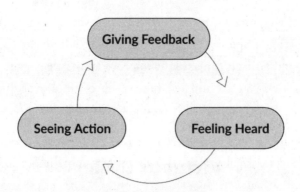

Trust Grows

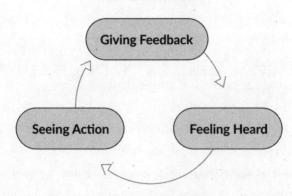

Trust Grows

I cannot stress enough how important it is to quickly respond to feedback with meaningful action. This not only builds trust. It can, in and of itself, dramatically improve employee engagement and retention.

Research from Gallup has found that **engagement is nearly three times higher** in organizations when employees strongly agree with the statement:

"My organization acts upon the results of surveys I complete."

A Game-Changing System for Inspiring Greatness (Employee Engagement)

The process recommended in Part 1 provides a simple, clear solution to the issues that have resulted in the average level of employee engagement not improving in the last twenty years. By following this process, your team or organization will avoid the pitfalls of measuring the wrong variables (perks and benefits), offering leadership training that makes little or no lasting impact, or responding to employee feedback slowly. Instead, your team or organization will be focused on helping direct managers inspire greatness in their teams (the most important driver of engagement), it will offer leadership training in a way that creates lasting transformation, and it will be empowered to respond to feedback with meaningful action almost instantly.

Just by using surveys in synchronization with leadership development, which allows you to quickly respond to feedback with leadership training that inspires leaders to act on the most highly leveraged behaviors for driving high levels of employee engagement, you'll be able to scale a sustainable, high-performance culture that makes a bigger impact on the customers you serve. In other words, you'll be able to consistently inspire greatness by helping team members to thrive.

You'll also be able to provide leadership training that is more than just a nice perk and another expense, as it tends to be in many organizations. Leadership training will become one of the best investments you can make.

According to the most recent research published by Gallup (a meta-analysis that included over 100,000 business units and actually compared business units to other units in the same company to control as many variables as possible), organizations in the top 25 percent of employee engagement levels are 18 percent more productive (as measured by sales) than those in the bottom 25 percent. This is because improving employee engagement improves the effectiveness of salespeople, as well as product quality and customer service, all of which affect top-line revenue.

Based on the data above, and other publicly available data from Gallup regarding the employee engagement levels of the bottom- and top-quartile companies, I believe a very conservative estimate is that for every ten out of one hundred employees that an organization can move from not engaged (or actively disengaged) to engaged, it would realize a 3.3 percent increase in top-line revenue.

In other words, if a company that generates $100 million in annual revenue could move just ten out of every one hundred employees from not engaged to engaged, it would likely add $3.3 million to its top-line revenue. And Gallup's most recent data shows that companies in the top quartile of employee engagement levels also have 23 percent higher net profit margins than those in the bottom quartile. This is because improving employee engagement reduces turnover, shrinkage, absenteeism, and safety incidents, all of which reduces costs. Thus, the company above that added $3.3 million to its top-line revenue would also likely keep significantly more of the added revenue as net profit.

Helping ten out of every one hundred employees move from not engaged to engaged is fairly easy to achieve with the approach outlined in this book. Organizations that apply this approach often have more than double the levels of employee engagement compared to organizations that fail to quickly respond to employee feedback with meaningful action from direct managers. Thus, even if the company above invested $330,000 to create the increase in employee engagement, it would realize a tenfold, or 1,000 percent, return on that investment in terms of increased revenue alone.

Perhaps more important, in addition to improving business performance, if you help move employees from not engaged to engaged, you'll also be making a significant positive impact in the lives of your employees. You'll be helping those human beings to thrive, both professionally and personally, which can in turn make a significant positive impact on both the local and global communities.

• • • Action Item for Chapter 4 • • •

Please write out a plan, based on the guidance in this chapter, for how you and/or your leaders will have training sessions ready to go before surveys are deployed so you can take meaningful action on the feedback you receive from your direct reports within a few days of receiving that feedback.

Summary of Part 1

Step 1—Implement a system for frequently reminding leaders that their primary job and top priority is to inspire greatness (engagement) in team members.

- Even the best leaders (like Garry Ridge) benefit from frequent reminders about what matters most.
- This meta habit helps create other habits for consistently inspiring greatness in others.
- This also helps reinforce the important fact that ultimate responsibility for employee engagement rests with leaders, not HR. Engagement isn't an HR thing. It's a leadership thing.

Step 2—Identify the needs people have for thriving—being happy, great human beings who do great work—focusing on the universal needs most strongly correlated with employee engagement.

- By focusing on the most important drivers of employee engagement instead of things like perks and benefits, the effectiveness of engagement initiatives is dramatically improved.

Step 3—Get regular feedback, in small, digestible bits, on how well direct managers are meeting the needs people have for thriving, focusing on the universal needs most strongly correlated with employee engagement.

- Because 70 percent of employee engagement is driven by direct managers, this helps make the biggest impact the fastest. HR and other leaders can get feedback on org-wide issues later.
- By getting feedback in small, digestible bits, it's easier for employees to provide feedback.
- By focusing on universal needs first, engagement efforts are most highly leveraged. Managers and HR teams can work to uncover and meet unique needs later on.

Step 4—Accompany feedback to managers with brief training (ideally either live or via videos) that helps them immediately act on employee feedback and develop simple, sticky habits for meeting the needs people have for thriving (the needs for realizing greatness).

- By offering training in small, digestible bits with lots of time for implementation in between training sessions, it's much more likely that leadership training will result in ideas turning into new behaviors that are repeated and become lasting habits.
- By synchronizing training with employee feedback, employees see meaningful action being taken on their feedback in a matter of days. This alone can nearly triple employee engagement compared to organizations that don't respond well to feedback.

A Special Gift

At this point, there's a good chance that you are thinking, *The four-step process outlined in Part 1 sounds awesome, but it sounds like there's a lot of up-front work involved to get it started.*

Well, here is some very good news for you!

It's possible to fully automate the entire four-step process using existing technology and training videos, and have this entire system up and running in just a few hours.

And I'd be happy to provide you with a free consultation to show you exactly how to do this.

The free, forty-five-minute consultation will include the following outcomes:

1. We'll get a clear picture of your current needs and capabilities.
2. We'll answer any questions you have about the process and how to customize it for your team or organization.
3. You'll leave the consultation with a customized plan for quickly automating the four-step process you learned in this book.

At this point, you may be wondering, *Why on earth would you just give away such valuable consulting time?*

That's a great question. The answer has two parts:

1. The top priority for my team and me is making an impact and making our vision of the future a reality.

   We envision a world in which all leaders and workplace cultures consistently make a positive impact on the growth and well-being of team members. We believe this would create the conditions for a permanent end to poverty, violence, and other unnecessary suffering in the world.

   If you want to apply our system on your own, you'll be helping us realize our vision.

2. My team and I have created a software tool that automates the entire four-step process that you learn about in this book. The software tool automates the delivery of all the surveys, feedback emails, and training videos we've made for the customers who use our tool.

   We know that some of the people we help with a free consultation will decide that instead of building their own program in house, they would rather use the software solution we've built. And people who use our software solution not only help us realize our vision, they also help us financially justify the free consulting time we're offering.

To be clear, I'm happy to help either way because either way helps us realize our vision.

And either way helps you and the leaders on your team to more consistently meet the needs of employees so that you can dramatically improve employee engagement, realize a sustainable, high-performance culture, and live a more meaningful life.

If you'd like to schedule a free consultation, please do one of the following:

1. Visit the webpage—inspiregreatnessbook.com/gift.

   or

2. Text the word "gift" to me at 615-645-3303 and I'll send you a link where you can schedule a call at your convenience.

PART 2

Building the Habits That Inspire Greatness

How to Use Part 2
of This Book

I n this part of the book, each chapter is going to include more details on one of the fourteen universal needs people have for thriving at work (listed again below), which are most strongly correlated with high levels of engagement and retention, along with a couple of habits for consistently meeting the need addressed in the chapter.

The first time you read Part 2, I recommend reading it for enjoyment and inspiration—without taking action on the action items—at whatever pace is comfortable for you. My hope is that this will further inspire you to act on the information in this book and help you develop lasting habits for consistently inspiring greatness in your team members.

The second time you read Part 2, I recommend you read one chapter at a time, following the action items at the end of each chapter, and committing to working on only one new habit at a time, for at least two weeks, before starting to work on the next one. For some leaders, especially those who still perform a lot of individual contributor–type tasks, three or four weeks between new habits might be more realistic. What's most important is to find the right pace that will allow you to stick with new behaviors so that they become lasting habits.

For instance, the first habit, which you learned about in chapter two, is to read aloud your new job description at least three times a day for the next thirty days. After your first read-through of Part 2, I recommend that you wait at least two weeks (or three or four if need be) from the time you began the first new habit before you start working on the habit you'll learn about in chapter five.

Two weeks after you started working on the foundational habit from chapter two (reading your new job description), you may want to reread chapter five for inspiration, then begin working on the action items at the end of the chapter.

Then wait two weeks and reread chapter six, and start working on one more habit, and so on.

This approach will help you achieve two important goals:

First, when you read this book straight through the first time, you may think you couldn't possibly perform all of the action items. It's true that, if you tried to do them all in a month, you almost certainly couldn't perform all of the action items. However, by taking just a few minutes every two or three weeks to automate the process with calendar events and reminders, over the course of twelve months or so, you'll find that you absolutely can develop most, if not all, of the habits suggested in this book.

Second, this approach will help ensure that you don't fall into the trap I mentioned in chapter four. Please don't just allow the inspiration I hope this book gives you to fade away without taking action. Instead, take action in small, digestible chunks that will help you transform information and inspiration into lasting habits that help you consistently inspire greatness in your team members and live a more meaningful and fulfilling life.

Fourteen Universal Needs for Thriving at Work

1. **Appreciation/Recognition:** People need to feel recognized and/or appreciated so they know they are making a contribution.

2. **Autonomy:** People need to feel that they have as much control as possible over their lives.

3. **Belonging:** People need to feel that they are part of a group with mutual respect and care, and shared values.

4. **Clarity of Expectations:** A lack of clarity is a significant source of anxiety and frustration.

5. **Doing Work That Leverages Strengths:** The more time people spend doing work they enjoy and are good at, the more likely they are to be engaged.

6. **Excellence:** People inherently want and need to do a great job.

7. **Feedback:** People need regular, helpful feedback.

8. **Feeling Like One's Opinion Matters / Is Heard:** People need to feel like their ideas matter.

9. **Feeling Cared For by One's Manager:** This is the most powerful driver of engagement, and the foundation for meeting all other needs. People need to know that their manager cares about them as a person and works to help them be a happy, great human being who does great work.

10. **Growth:** People need to be continuously growing.

11. **Having the Tools Required to Do One's Job:** Lacking the tools to do one's job is a significant source of anxiety and frustration.

12. **Meaningful Work:** People need to find meaning at work.

13. **Trust:** People need to know that they can trust their coworkers, most importantly their leaders.

14. **Well-Being:** People need to be able to go to work without adverse effects on their physical and emotional well-being.

5

Facilitating Excellence

One Secret for Simultaneously Meeting Individual and Organizational Needs

After graduating with degrees in accounting and economics, Aaron Anderson entered the workforce right out of college with what many in his position would consider a dream job at Deloitte. He worked hard and was promoted several times in a matter of a few years. It was clear he was on track to becoming a partner.

Although the idea of being a partner was certainly alluring to him, Aaron also wanted to be the best husband and father he could be, and he knew that being a partner at a large firm was likely going to make it more difficult to serve his family as well as he aspired to. So, he decided to pursue a different path. After nearly a decade with Deloitte, Aaron went to work for IBM.

Although his initial intent was to work as an individual contributor in a technical role, Aaron soon found himself being promoted to a director role. Shortly after that, he was asked to head up a new department that would focus on helping IBM better comply with international accounting standards, since ever-increasing amounts of the company's business occurred internationally.

Aaron was consistently excellent in his career, and being excellent added significantly to his fulfillment in life. But he felt something was missing, that there was something more fulfilling out there.

Tara, Aaron's colleague, had been at IBM for twenty-five years. She was the proud mother of three children. Her career began on the fast track, and she had been promoted as a result. Her next promotion would be to a director-level position.

A couple years went by. Then a few more. The promotion never came.

Tara had apparently plateaued. For some reason, perhaps only because she was a woman in an industry traditionally dominated by men, no one thought that she was talented enough to be promoted. After ten years at this plateau, even Tara started to doubt that she was talented enough to be promoted.

When Aaron Anderson approached Tara and asked her to join the new team he was building, her reply was, "Why would you want me? You need highly talented people like you."

Aaron saw things differently, though. He explained that since he had only been at IBM—an extremely complex organization—for three years, he needed someone like Tara, who had been with the company for a long time.

He also told her that he believed she was one of the smartest people he had ever met, and that he needed someone like her to help solve some of the complex issues the team would be addressing. Tara reluctantly agreed to join the team.

Within a matter of months, she was thriving. She was no longer just executing the same technical tasks month after month after month. The new role gave her the opportunity to apply her amazing intellect to think strategically and solve complex problems.

About eighteen months after Tara joined Aaron's team, Aaron was invited to present on a panel of chief accounting officers at a large conference. He noticed that all the other panel members were women, so he asked Tara to present instead.

Tara initially said, "No way!"

She knew that everyone else on the panel was a chief accounting officer at a large company, and she wasn't even a director.

Aaron said, "Tara, they may be chief accounting officers, but I know that you'll be the smartest, most talented person on that panel. You'll be amazing."

Tara reluctantly agreed to present on the panel. She and Aaron spent many hours preparing for the event. Aaron would often invite Tara to debate ideas with him. She not only did well in the debates, she would often win them.

Because she had so much respect for Aaron's intellect, the debates helped her start to believe in herself more and more. Nevertheless, right up to the day before the event, Tara expressed concerns that she shouldn't be up there, and would likely not do well.

The day of the event finally arrived. Aaron sat in the front row to watch Tara and support her, if needed.

As the panel wrapped up, Aaron wanted to go speak with Tara about how she did, but he couldn't. Although all of the other panelists were nearby and available for conversations with people who had been in the audience, none of the other panelists had anyone approaching them.

Everyone was rushing to talk to Tara. She had absolutely crushed it.

Nearly an hour later, when all the people waiting to speak with Tara had either spoken to her or left to attend another session, Aaron finally got his chance to speak with her.

He asked, "You were the smartest person up there, weren't you?"

He could see it in her eyes. She believed she was.

Several years later, Aaron was confident that his team no longer needed him and he left to take on a new challenge at MasterCard. Although it didn't happen right away, Tara was offered a promotion to be a director, and the head of the team at IBM that she and Aaron had created. Unfortunately for IBM, Tara had already accepted a director role at another company by the time she was finally offered the director role at IBM.

People Want to Be Excellent

A universal need shared by every healthy human is the need to be good, or even great, at what we do. This, of course, is very good news for leaders. The fact that people are wired to want to be excellent means our goals for operational excellence are ultimately aligned with the individual goals of team members to be excellent in their roles.

Clearly, no one wants to be bad at things they do regularly. Could you imagine a person who wakes up in the morning and says the following?

"Today, I aspire to be . . . mediocre. And not just today. But every day for the rest of my life!"

The idea that someone would say something like this is absurd, isn't it? Nevertheless, we see mediocre people everywhere. Why is this?

I used to think that individuals were entirely responsible for whether or not they were successful in life. However, there is little evidence to support that view. There is, however, an abundance of evidence suggesting that a person's environment, and the habits that are created by that environment, are almost entirely (if not entirely) responsible for the success or failure of teams and individuals.

There's a terrible conundrum with habits, which, I believe, is why we see so many people who are consistently mediocre at work, or in other areas of their lives. The conundrum is this: bad habits are easy to form and hard to break, and good habits are hard to form and easy to break.

For example, let's say you want to run a marathon, so you're trying to build the habit of running six days per week. What's easier, to get up immediately when the alarm goes off, go to the bathroom, get dressed, and go for a ten-mile run in the cold, or to reach over and hit the SNOOZE button?

Not only is hitting SNOOZE easier, but it provides an immediate, pleasurable experience. So it goes with almost every habit.

Bad habits are easy to form because they are almost always easier to start, and almost always provide an immediate experience of pleasure.

Good habits are very hard to form because they are harder to start, and they almost never provide immediate positive results or pleasure. In fact, good habits often provide an unpleasant experience in the short term. Although I personally really like running overall, and have been running two to five days per week consistently for over twenty-five years, I still find the first few minutes of running to be unpleasant.

There's good news (that initially appears to be bad news) regarding the idea that whether people are consistently mediocre or excellent is almost entirely a function of their habits. This situation creates a tremendous opportunity for leaders.

Because bad habits are easy to form and hard to break, and good habits are hard to form and easy to break, most people find it very difficult to break bad habits and form and maintain good habits on their own. Thus, if you can make the shift to more consistently serving as a coach whose primary job is to inspire greatness, you can help people identify and overcome bad habits and thus meet a very important human need (the need to be excellent) that is very difficult to meet on their own.

If you work to help people be excellent because you care about them and you want to help them realize greater satisfaction and fulfillment in life, people will feel that care, and deeply appreciate it. Think of someone in your life who invested time and energy in helping you be the best you could be in some area of your life. How much gratitude do you feel for that person?

Sometimes helping people to overcome the obstacles to being excellent can be simple. In the story of Tara and Aaron Anderson, all Tara needed was someone who believed in her to help remove her doubts and restore her self-confidence. As Aaron continued to speak and act in ways that demonstrated that he truly did believe she was talented, she began to believe in herself again, too.

In other cases, there might be more work involved to help people overcome habits that are keeping them from reaching their potential. But investing time and energy in the effort to help a team member to be excellent is one of the best investments leaders can make. A simple habit that facilitates the process of helping team members to be consistently excellent is the habit of regular one-to-one meetings.

The Power of One-to-Ones

For many managers, when they first learn about the importance of having regular one-to-one meetings with team members, they immediately feel resistance to the idea. So, if you're feeling resistance, don't worry. It's very normal.

Managers are often the most overworked employees in an organization, and they often find it difficult to imagine finding the time to have regular one-to-one meetings with team members, or making time for more frequent one-to-one meetings. But regular one-to-one meetings are among the most highly leveraged activities that managers can engage in. The list of benefits of regular one-to-one meetings is almost endless, so I'll focus on just a few here.

Putting time on the calendar to invest in one-to-one meetings with team members, and doing whatever we can to make sure we meet at the scheduled time, sends a very strong message to team members that we truly care about them. And, if they're done well, one-to-one meetings will save you a lot of time and make your work as a manager much more enjoyable and rewarding. That's right, regular one-to-one meetings will actually save you time in the long run.

If you're a manager, you're going to spend a lot of time helping employees and dealing with employee issues, at least for a while. That's nonnegotiable if you want to have any success as a leader. The question is, how do you want to spend that time?

Do you want to spend the time on the back end, reacting to things, running around like a chicken with your head cut off, doing stuff that sucks, or would you like to spend the time up front doing things that are enjoyable?

If managers don't regularly meet with team members, what tends to happen is that small problems go unaddressed and become big problems. Then, managers spend a lot of time doing things that are painful, like putting out fires, losing good employees, and having to recruit new employees. Dealing with big problems is not only painful; it is very time consuming. In fact, it's these very activities that can transform being a manager into one of the most stressful jobs in the world.

But time spent having regular one-to-one meetings actually makes work as a manager much more enjoyable. This is where you get to have quality conversations with team members that make a positive impact in their professional and personal lives and discover some of the unique needs team members have for thriving at work. And, ironically, by investing that time up front, managers can actually end up saving time because regular, proactive, quality meetings with team members takes significantly less time than reacting to big problems like losing a good employee and having to scramble to replace that person.

Here's what I recommend to start taking advantage of the power of one-to-ones. If you're not currently having one-to-one meetings, start scheduling at least one of them each month with each team member for a minimum of twenty minutes.

In an ideal world, managers whose team members are doing complex thought work should be having one-to-one meetings with every team member every week. For managers whose team members are doing less complex work, like warehouse work or entry-level work, having one-to-ones once every two to three weeks may suffice. But for any manager with more than ten direct reports, or who is still performing a lot of individual contributor tasks, these levels of frequency may be challenging.

If you can only do a single one-to-one meeting per month for now, that's okay. But as you start realizing how valuable one-to-one meetings are, you might try to delegate more individual contributor tasks to your team members (you'll learn more about delegation in chapter fourteen). If you have more than fifteen direct reports, you might even consider creating one or more team lead positions, and allowing those team leaders to conduct one-to-one meetings with a small number of team members.

If you're going to be doing one meeting per month, I recommend splitting the meeting into two parts. Half of the meeting can be about work performance, if needed. The other half should be about helping the team member to thrive, both professionally and personally.

If you're doing at least two meetings per month, I recommend having one meeting about work performance and one devoted entirely to helping the team member to thrive, both professionally and personally. When you're talking about performance, your objective should be to serve as a coach who is helping team members to be the best version of themselves possible. As you learned in chapter two, you will be much more effective if your motivation for helping people do great work is not to benefit you, but to benefit them.

You could start off by asking what team members feel they have done well since the last meeting, and add your thoughts afterwards. You could then ask them to share any areas where they felt stuck or feel that they didn't do as well as they'd like to, and add your thoughts afterward, if necessary. Then you could ask what they plan on doing to improve in that area, and if there's anything you can do to help them achieve their goals.

In the time devoted to helping them thrive, you could ask questions like . . .

- Is there anything I could do to remove obstacles for you or help make your work more enjoyable?
- What are you most excited about outside of work?
- Is there anything you're struggling with outside of work that you think I could help with?

The last question in the list above provides a simple way to discover unique needs team members have that you could help address.

Warning: An Addiction to Inspiring Greatness May Develop

Although getting regular one-to-ones on the calendar and showing up for them can be initially challenging, and even a little painful, much like starting a running habit, I am very confident that you'll start to enjoy the process immediately, in your first one-to-one, by following the approach outlined in this chapter. Over time, you'll enjoy regular, quality one-to-ones even more, as well as the impacts they have on both the performance and well-being of your team members. In fact, you might develop an addiction to inspiring excellence, in much the same way runners often get addicted to running.

This is precisely what happened to Aaron Anderson after he helped Tara get promoted to a director role at IBM. As much as he used to love the thrill of individual achievement and personal excellence, he realized that inspiring greatness in others was significantly more rewarding.

As an individual contributor, he worked to be the best he could be at his job. As a leader, he discovered that the most rewarding endeavor was to work himself out of a job, and he became addicted to it. For the remainder of his career, his goal was to help team members to do and be their best, and develop people into leaders who would eventually make Aaron redundant.

For new leaders, or those aspiring to be leaders, this can sound scary. People often think that if they were to develop their teams to the point where they, as managers, are no longer needed, they will literally be out of a job.

However, this rarely happens. In most cases, when senior leaders see that a manager has developed the team to the point where the manager is no longer needed, those senior leaders do not think, *I guess we should let the manager go.* They think, *We need to promote that manager and give her more responsibility.*

In the rare case where that is not possible, and there is no position with greater responsibility at the manager's organization, that manager can easily find a more senior role someplace else. Leaders like this are highly valued in the marketplace.

When I interviewed Aaron Anderson for this book, he had worked himself out of several jobs, including at MasterCard and PayPal. One of the people he had developed while working himself out of his most recent job was Tara. The director role she had accepted before she was finally offered the promotion at IBM was at PayPal.

Aaron Anderson had helped her land the role at PayPal. And when he was promoted after working himself out of another job, Tara helped fill the void. She was promoted to a senior director role there, too.

After developing people as much as he thought he could at PayPal, Aaron hadn't been offered an opportunity to make a bigger impact there, so he decided to step down.

I asked him, "Where will you be going?"

He replied, "I'm not sure yet, but I'll be looking for an opportunity to work myself out of another job."

Aaron is no longer concerned with income or status. He is addicted to inspiring greatness in others.

• • • Action Items for Chapter 5 • • •

1. Please schedule one-to-one meetings on your calendar right now, while it's fresh in your mind, per the guidance in this chapter, beginning two weeks after you started the habit of reading your new job description each day.

2. Please create an event on your calendar for some time before your next one-to-one to create a plan for how the meeting will go, per the guidance in this chapter.

6

Making Appreciation an Art

A Life-Changing Habit

The day before, I had delivered an eight-hour corporate training, and the client invited me to an evening celebration event. Despite feeling exhausted after leading a day of training, I knew it would mean a lot to the client if I attended, so I went.

I ended up staying later than I expected, and didn't get to bed until midnight. So, when I boarded the plane for my six-forty-five flight in the morning, I just wanted to go back to sleep. Nevertheless, I made sure to at least greet the person sitting next to me first.

My neighbor was a woman who I would estimate was in her early thirties with beautiful, dark brown skin, curly black hair in braids, and bright, engaging eyes. She was overflowing with positive energy. What I thought would be a quick conversation before going to sleep quickly transformed into one of the most inspiring interactions I've ever had.

When I shared how tired I was, my seatmate shared that she was exhausted, too. And, to recharge, she was going on vacation.

"Where are you going?" I asked.

She said, "I'm going to Haiti to do volunteer work."

"What type of volunteer work are you going to do in Haiti?" I asked.

"I'm going to donate medical exams to the people there," she replied.

"Oh, are you a nurse or a doctor?"

"I'm an emergency department physician," she said.

Although I have devoted most of my life to serving others and written much about the power of service, I was surprised that a physician would go on vacation to recharge and, instead of relaxing and recreating, would do the same thing that she's paid to do, but do it for free.

"So, on your vacation, to recharge, you're going to go do your job, but for no pay?" I asked.

"Yes," she replied. "But there's a big difference between the work I do in the emergency room here in the States and the work I do for the people in Haiti."

"What's the difference?" I asked.

"Let me give you an example of what my job is often like in an emergency room here in the States," she said. "A couple weeks ago, I was about nine hours into a twelve-hour shift. The emergency department was overflowing, so I had to move as quickly as possible to keep up and ensure that people didn't have to wait too long.

"I had gone nine hours without eating any food, drinking any water, or even going to the bathroom. I had spent the last three hours of that time working to save a six-month-old baby who had coded.

"After my team and I did everything we possibly could to save that baby's life, we lost her."

"Oh my," I said, finding it difficult to imagine how emotionally challenging that must have been.

She continued. "The family was devastated and so were my team and I. But we didn't have a moment to grieve. After spending as much time as possible being present with the family who just lost their baby, I had to go on to see the next patient.

"I read the chart before I walked in and realized that this was another of the many cases we see every day of people who really should not be in the emergency department. It was very likely that the family was abusing the emergency department with a non-serious health issue because they didn't have health insurance.

"All three people looked angry when I walked in the room and, with an angry tone, the first thing the woman in the room said was, 'Do you know we've been waiting for three hours? Why did you take so long?'

"I almost lost it. My mind raced with thoughts of how the day had gone. A potential reply raced through my mind as well. It was something like,

Do you realize that I have worked nine hours straight without eating food, drinking water, or going to the bathroom, and then just spent three hours working in vain to save a baby's life? And it's because of people like you who abuse our emergency department that we're overflowing with long wait times and sometimes can't save the lives of people who really need us?

"But I kept that response in my head. I took a deep breath and I replied, 'I'm very sorry that you had to wait so long. How can I be of help to you?'"

I realized that I was talking to a truly awesome human being. Although I have been teaching mindfulness for twenty years, and I've written a book on the topic, I am not sure I would have been able to respond in the way she did.

"That is absolutely incredible!" I said. "I can't believe that you were able to respond in such a compassionate way at that moment."

"Thank you," she replied. "I think the fact that I knew this trip was coming so soon helped me a lot in that situation."

"Really? So what makes serving as a physician in Haiti and not getting paid for it so much different than the work you do here in the emergency department in the States?"

She replied, "In Haiti, people often walk for hours and wait several hours more just to see me and get a simple checkup.

"All I'm doing is checking their vitals and asking them a few questions about their health. But these people are so grateful that, despite being among the poorest people on the planet, they often bring me gifts that either take them hours of their time to make or cost them a few days' worth of their salary.

"*That* is the difference. The appreciation that the people in Haiti show me for doing such simple things is so impactful that it recharges my spirit and empowers me to go do six months of work in the States before I need to come back for another recharge."

I could literally *feel* what she was talking about. I felt recharged just sitting next to her and receiving the positive energy she exuded, which seemed to have been created from her just anticipating the appreciation she would receive in Haiti.

The Power of Appreciation

Feeling appreciated is such an important need that people would do their jobs voluntarily if they felt appreciated enough. Of course, I'm not suggesting that we don't pay employees a fair salary. In fact, I'm pointing to something almost the opposite.

I've heard leaders push back against the idea of sharing appreciation with employees for doing their jobs. They say things like, "I'm paying them. Isn't that appreciation?"

No. It's not. Being paid for work is required by law unless a person specifically requests to be a volunteer.

It can be helpful to think of employees on your team as volunteers. They're not working on your team because they have to. They are "volunteering" to work on your team. They are choosing to work on your team. Unless a person has no education or skills of any kind, they can find many other employers who will meet the basic need of getting paid.

If you want to ensure that people don't choose to go find another employer who will meet the need of a paycheck, you need to meet other needs people have for thriving at work. Feeling appreciated is one of those needs. According to research from Gallup, employees who don't feel appreciated are twice as likely to leave in the following twelve months.

Effectively appreciating employees has numerous other business benefits as well, including increases in employee engagement that result in profound effects. According to Gallup, globally, only one out of every four employees strongly agrees that they have been recognized or appreciated for their contributions in the last seven days. And, by increasing that ratio to six out of ten, organizations could realize a 28 percent improvement in quality, a 31 percent reduction in absenteeism, and a 12 percent reduction in shrinkage.

When leaders consistently and effectively appreciate employees, team performance can significantly increase as well, especially by appreciating what we want to see more of. This inspires the team member we're appreciating, as well as the rest of the team, to repeat helpful and productive behaviors. This is much more effective than spending a lot of time criticizing mistakes or unwanted behaviors.

Perhaps most important, this is one of the most powerful ways to demonstrate that we care about the people on our teams, which is the most powerful driver of engagement. People who feel genuinely appreciated for their contributions tend to be among the most engaged, and loyal, team members.

Being a Leader People Want to Follow

Prior to joining Kraft Heinz, Amber had spent nearly a decade as a top performer at two other Fortune 1000 companies.

At the first company she joined, Amber had a boss who was extremely competitive and seemed to think that the best way to motivate people was to constantly tell them about everything they were doing wrong. Amber literally never received a single form of appreciation from her manager.

In fact, on one occasion, in a one-to-one meeting, Amber's manager told her that a person from another department had praised her. But instead of reading the email to Amber, her manager just quickly mentioned that Amber had received praise from a colleague, seemed to dismiss it as unimportant with a hand gesture, and quickly transitioned to telling Amber about areas she could improve. Amber started looking for a new job very quickly.

The manager at the next company Amber joined was very different. He said "Thank you" or "Good job" often. Amber noticed that, although he offered a lot of praise, he didn't offer any detail and he wasn't very specific about what he was appreciating, so it was hard for Amber to know what exactly she should be doing more of.

However, at the time, Amber didn't think much about the quality of the appreciation she received from her boss. It was just so refreshing to finally feel like her manager appreciated the work she did.

She thought about her past experiences as she read an email from Mark Smith, her manager and the global head of talent at Kraft Heinz. It was the third time in as many weeks that Amber had received an email from Mark with a detailed note thanking her for work she had recently done.

As she read the email, her first thought was, *Where does he find the time to do this stuff? After all, Mark is the global head of talent at a Fortune 500 company. He surely has a lot on his plate.*

The appreciation Amber received from Mark made such an emotional impact on her that she has kept all the emails in a folder labeled "Feel Good." In addition to making her happy, the emails have also boosted her confidence. She truly believes that she is talented and her performance has improved as a result.

Also, because the praise is very specific, Amber knows how to leverage her strengths. She knows exactly what she should be doing more of.

The positive impact Mark has already had on Amber is so profound that when I asked her if there was anything else she wanted to share about the impact Mark has made, she said, "I can tell you this. I love this company. I think it's great. But if Mark were to leave, I would do whatever I could to join his new team."

She wouldn't be the first to do this. Of the fifty people who currently report to Mark, five of them had worked with him at previous companies and, when Mark moved on, joined Mark's new team within a matter of months of him joining Kraft Heinz.

The Habit of Frequent Appreciation

If you are among the vast majority of managers who aren't showing appreciation often enough, the research suggests that you're clearly not alone. And you definitely shouldn't be too hard on yourself about this. We humans are not naturally wired to be good at seeing what things are going right. We tend to overly focus on what's going wrong.

It's fairly easy to see why this is the case. For the vast majority of our evolutionary history, we lived in environments that were filled with life-threatening danger. In order to survive as a species, we needed to be very good at seeing what's wrong.

If you're walking through the woods and you fail to notice a good potential mate, the chances are very high that you'll come across another potential good mate some other time. But if you fail to notice soon enough that a predator is stalking you, you'll never have another chance at procreation.

It's only been in the last few thousand years that we've been able to remove ourselves from the constant threats found in nature. So our brains are still hardwired to scan for the negative. The good news is that the brain is very plastic. It is malleable.

It is now well known that we can create new neural networks, and even new neurons, up until the day we die. While it is true that the brain changes more slowly as we age, it still changes.

We can break the habit of over-focusing on the negative and get better at seeing what's going well in our environment. And getting better at this is a meta habit, or what Charles Duhigg calls a "keystone habit," which is a habit that makes many other good habits much easier to form.

The habit of seeing and appreciating what's right can help us help our team members to thrive, and drive high levels of engagement and sustainable high performance. And, as we get better at seeing what's right in our lives, and expressing gratitude for it, our lives improve in a number of areas. In fact, some researchers, like Andrew Huberman, who is a neurobiology professor at the Stanford University School of Medicine, believe that daily gratitude practices may be the most impactful practices for realizing both professional success and satisfaction in life.

Here's what I recommend for rewiring your brain to see more of what's right, and offering more frequent appreciation for team members. First, create an event on your calendar with a pop-up and email notification that best fits into your workflow, for some time toward the end of the day. This event should be on your calendar every day for the next thirty workdays.

The reminder in the notification should be this:

Reflect back on the day and think of at least one person who did something right, and thank them for it as soon as possible.

It's important to be specific regarding what you're appreciating. For instance, instead of saying something generic like "Great job!" you might communicate:

You handled that customer complaint very well. I noticed you really listened well and made her feel heard, and you found a great solution to her problem. This is extremely important for helping our organization create happy customers who keep coming back and telling other people about us, which is the most effective marketing there is. Thank you very much for taking such good care of her, Susan.

If you can do this for thirty days, you may not need the calendar reminder anymore. You will have formed a new habit that has the potential to change your life, and the lives of your team members. You could also ask your team members to join you in this effort to help build a team culture of appreciation, which can help team members feel even more appreciated at work without any additional effort from you.

The Art of Appreciation

After you develop the habit of showing appreciation more frequently, you can build on that habit by making your appreciation even more impactful. Following are some ideas for transforming appreciation into an art form.

First, it's important that daily appreciation for small wins be shared as soon as possible after the event occurs.

Second, it's important to share appreciation in a way that the team member will best receive it. As my colleague Shane Green pointed out to me in a podcast interview, many managers say that they're sharing appreciation with team members all the time. Yet most of those same team members will often say they rarely, if ever, receive appreciation.

Shane points out that the primary reason for this is that people receive and process information in different ways. Very few people process information using only their auditory sense. So, if all of our appreciation consists only of verbally sharing a "Thank you," most people aren't going to process that well, and they won't feel appreciated.

Many people process information primarily through the visual or kinesthetic senses, or some combination of the visual, kinesthetic, and auditory senses. So, if we want to ensure team members feel truly appreciated, we need to share appreciation in the ways they're most likely to process.

In the case of people doing little things right, a detailed email could be enough to help people process via the visual sense. For bigger wins, a handwritten note delivered or mailed in an envelope the team member has to open could be enough to help them process through both the visual and kinesthetic senses. For cases where people go above and beyond the call of duty, you might want to take them to lunch, or buy them a virtual lunch if you're virtual, give them a written thank-you card, and verbally thank them over the lunch.

If you want to take this a step further, and transform appreciation into an art form, I recommend you take some time to customize the appreciation for the individual, based on what you know is important to him, particularly if he has consistently exceeded expectations.

You can rely on what you know is important to the team member to customize it. During onboarding or one-to-one meetings, you could also ask the team member how she likes to be recognized or appreciated. For instance, an extrovert might like to be recognized in front of team members. But for an introvert, that might seem like punishment.

Customizing appreciation in this way can make a huge impact. Here's an example for you.

A colleague and friend of mine, named John Spence, is recognized as one of the top business thought leaders in the world, and has been the CEO of several organizations. He once had an administrative assistant on his team who consistently exceeded expectations, for years.

He wanted to do something big to show her how much he appreciated her. He knew that nothing in her life was more important to her than her husband and children. So John wrote a letter by hand. He sent it to the husband and asked him to read it out loud to her in front of the children.

In the letter, John detailed all the ways she was amazing, and such a valuable asset to his team, and thanked her profusely. He also thanked the husband and children for giving her time to work on his team.

I can easily imagine her crying, as her husband read this letter, which she apparently did. I mentioned to John a few years ago that I had been sharing this story about him. He said, "What a coincidence. I just spoke with her last week. She brought up that letter on the call, and how much it impacted her."

After fifteen years, she still remembered that experience like it was yesterday. This is the impact you can make by putting a little bit of thought into customizing appreciation. It cost John nothing but a few minutes of his time, and a stamp.

• • • Action Items for Chapter 6 • • •

1. Create a calendar event with notifications, per the guidance in this chapter, to catch at least one person doing something right every day. The goal should be to help each team member receive some type of appreciation at least once every workweek.
2. Let your team members know what you're working on and why, and invite them to develop the same habit to help increase their own happiness and help build a culture of appreciation on the team.

7

Providing Clear Expectations

How to Replace Frustration with Engagement

During the Christmas season of 2010, a Trader Joe's employee who we'll call Amanda received a phone call from a woman who was concerned about her eighty-nine-year-old father. He tended not to keep much food in the house and was essentially snowed in after a recent storm.

The man said a day without food wouldn't hurt him, but his daughter wasn't okay with that, and knew it wouldn't be safe for him to go out on his own after the storm. So, she called several stores to ask if they would deliver groceries to her father's house. She couldn't find one. Eventually, she called the Trader Joe's in Wayne, Pennsylvania, and explained the situation to Amanda.

As of this writing, the leaders at Trader Joe's have intentionally avoided the trend of delivering groceries. They have experimented with delivery with their New York stores, but found that it just wasn't a fit for them. It's expensive to create the infrastructure for deliveries. And a huge part of what makes Trader Joe's so special is the unique in-store experience that includes friendly staff dressed in Hawaiian-style shirts because they are "traders on the culinary seas, searching the world over for cool items to bring home to our customers."

Nevertheless, when Amanda heard about the situation of the eighty-nine-year-old man who was snowed in with no food in his house, she told the man's daughter that she'd be happy to deliver groceries to his house. The woman gratefully began reading to Amanda a list of grocery items, and mentioned that he was on a low-sodium diet. Amanda wrote down everything on the list, and even made some suggestions that would be good fits for a low-sodium diet.

Once Amanda had the list completed, the woman asked how she could pay. Amanda said, "Merry Christmas," and that there was no need to pay. Thirty minutes later, she arrived at the man's house with a few days' worth of food.

This story spread quickly on the online forum Reddit and was eventually discovered by Trader Joe's. One might expect that managers wouldn't be very happy with Amanda's decision to ignore a company policy and give away a few days' worth of food for free.

But the leaders at Trader Joe's didn't seem concerned at all. A representative of Trader Joe's wrote in the forum, "We are not quite sure which employee did this, but we will be in contact shortly so that you can personally thank him/her. We encourage this type of service at all our locations across the states."

After doing some research, the Trader Joe's representative updated the post with, "The person in question is a little hesistant [sic] to have their name on the internet. Send thanks to: 171 E Swedesford Rd, Wayne, PA 19087."

The reason that leaders at Trader Joe's were actually happy about Amanda's decision is that she was living two of the core values that guide decisions for everyone in the company: *Wow customer service* and *No bureaucracy*.

Amanda clearly delivered "wow" customer service. Both the woman and her father were likely absolutely amazed that Amanda delivered free food, appropriate for a low-sodium diet, in less-than-ideal driving conditions, to an elderly man in need. Thousands of people shared this story, resulting in lots of word-of-mouth marketing for Trader Joe's.

Also, Amanda felt safe to ignore a couple of company policies in this case because she knew that the leaders at Trader Joe's have made it clear that they don't want red tape to get in the way of delivering "wow" customer service.

Whether or not you agree with Trader Joe's approach to empowering frontline team members to make decisions on their own like the one Amanda made, there is a valuable lesson to be learned from this example. Apparently, it is clear to her what is expected of her at work.

The Power of Clear Expectations

Clarity around expectations may be the most foundational need for people to thrive and be engaged at work. I would guess that most leaders don't spend much time ensuring that expectations are clear because most leaders probably think that they have already made expectations clear.

However, research from Gallup has found that only half of employees strongly agree that they know what is expected of them. This, of course, is highly problematic.

A lack of clarity around expectations creates mediocrity, anxiety, and frustration for both managers and team members. According to Gallup, by increasing the percentage of employees who strongly agree that they know what is expected of them from 50 to 80 percent, teams and organizations could realize a 22 percent reduction in turnover, a 29 percent reduction in safety incidents, and a 10 percent increase in productivity (sales).

A lack of clarity can result in a lot of wasted time. Imagine a team member who is very excited and energized about doing great work and helping the organization realize its goals but, because the team member is not clear on what is expected, a lot of time ends up being wasted working on the wrong things. Or the team member makes a poor decision due to a lack of clarity around priorities or values.

Although clear communication is important in all relationships and interactions, in this chapter we'll focus on three touch points between managers and team members that are highly leveraged, and will allow you to create the most impact in the least amount of time:

1. Role clarity
2. Clarity on how to behave
3. Task clarity

Let's start with role clarity.

Role Clarity

An important first step for any manager is to lay out basic expectations for team members regarding what their roles are. In larger organizations, the task for creating and updating job descriptions is generally handled by HR. However, even in organizations with HR teams, it's important for direct managers to be involved, especially in terms of regularly updating job descriptions, as needed.

Having a job description that accurately reflects day-to-day responsibilities may seem like an administrative, "check-the-box" type of activity with no serious impact on performance. However, according to Gallup, employees who strongly agree that their job description aligns with the work they do are *more than twice as likely to be engaged* as are other employees.

Clarity on How to Behave

In addition to knowing "what" they should be doing, as outlined in their job descriptions, team members need to have clarity regarding "how" they should behave. This is partly because, in the grand scheme of things, both in business and in life in general, what we achieve is not as important as how we treat each other along the way. When we're too focused on performance, on the "what," it becomes easier for otherwise good people, while striving to hit a short-term goal, to behave in ways that are bad for the organization over the long term.

The efforts to clarify how to behave can include an informal discussion on what the culture is like and anything from how to dress to how formal or informal are the relationships between managers and employees. It can also include more formal things such as timeliness and standards of excellence.

I highly recommend you also take the time to share why these expectations are important. I recommend framing them, as much as possible, in the context of how meeting these expectations will help team members succeed professionally and in terms of developing healthy relationships with other team members.

A powerful practice is to ensure that you go beyond just outlining minimum expectations. You should also share what top performers are doing. I recommend letting team members know that you're going to help them to perform at a high level, too, so they can feel like they're making a great contribution to the team, enjoy their work more, and be more successful in their careers. This focus on excellence as a benefit for the team member is much more inspiring and energizing than focusing on what we want as managers.

Another important element of clarifying expectations around how to behave is having clearly written core values that are communicated often, starting with the onboarding experience. Larger organizations often have formal policies for various aspects of employment. But policies are more effective as a legal protection for the organization than they are for guiding the day-to-day behaviors of team members. A more effective approach to guiding day-to-day behaviors of team members is to really drill down and clearly define the core values of the organization.

When team members are clear on what the core values are for their team or organization, and on how to use those values to aid in decision-making, they are much more likely to make great decisions on their own. In the story about Amanda, from Trader Joe's, it's clear that she knew two of the core values of the company are *Wow customer service* and *No bureaucracy*. Because she also knew that those values should guide her decisions, she did something to delight a customer that many employees, in organizations with less clarity around values, would be afraid to do.

It's possible that your organization doesn't have core values identified, or the values are not written as well as they could be. In either of those cases, the first action item for this topic is to schedule a meeting with the management team to identify and write out your core values.

Here are a couple quick suggestions to help you write out or improve your current list of values. First, try to narrow down the list to just the absolute most important values, ideally about five, and no more than seven. Any more than that, and people won't remember them, so they won't be effective for guiding day-to-day behavior.

These should be the most important behaviors for driving healthy relationships and long-term success. In addition to being used to clarify how current team members should behave, these values can also serve to help identify whether a potential new hire will be a good fit for your team or organization.

Second, the values should include a brief description of each value, ideally just one sentence, as well as easy-to-measure behaviors that demonstrate whether the value is being lived.

For instance, many organizations say they value integrity. What does that mean? I would guess that if you asked five different people, you would get at least three different answers.

To clarify, you could describe the behaviors that demonstrate this value is being lived. For example, here are the integrity-related behaviors we measure in the organizations I've founded:

- I do what I say I'm going to do, even if it's hard.
- I tell the truth, even if it results in short-term loss for me or the company.
- I do not compromise my values or the company's core values for short-term gain.

By listing out the behaviors associated with each value, it becomes easier for the core values to guide behavior, and for leaders to measure whether or not people are living them.

Once your team has taken the time necessary to clearly list your core values, it's important to find ways to ensure that all team members understand these values. Ideally, team members should be able to state the core values from memory, at least in their own words.

Task Clarity

Although it's essential to create clarity around job descriptions, managers often assign short-term tasks and projects as well. It's very important to be clear here. I recommend two behaviors, which are relatively easy to turn into habits.

First, I recommend taking the time to share how a task fits into the strategic plan for the team or organization. This helps ensure that a team member understands why they are doing the task, which can help boost retention of the details of the task and improve engagement in its execution. This also helps team members to have more flexibility in terms of how they accomplish the task assigned, further increasing engagement and creating space for process improvements.

Second, I recommend getting unambiguous confirmation that a team member understands a task or project, and how it fits into the bigger picture, before any work begins.

Of course, one element of clarity is your ability to communicate in a way that is easy to understand, remember, and act on. If you often get feedback that people don't understand your communication, it could be a sign that you need to take more time to simplify and organize your communication before sending it out or before speaking with someone.

But communication is a two-way street. What might be clear to one team member may not be clear to another.

It is perfectly natural to assume that you are communicating clearly. When something makes sense in our own minds, we are likely to think it is clear in the minds of others. And, if we only ask one follow-up question after we've set an expectation or assigned a task, like "Do you understand?" or "Does that make sense?" we almost always get confirmation on that assumption. However, as you have probably experienced, people very often say they understand when, in fact, the idea they have in their mind is not the same as the idea you have in yours.

These types of misunderstandings have resulted in wasted time, losing customers, patients receiving the wrong medications, surgeries being performed on the wrong limbs or organs, buildings being incorrectly constructed, and even catastrophic accidents with public transportation. This is why it is so important to ask someone to explain in their own words what they understand.

One option for skillfully requesting this without insinuating that the team member wasn't paying attention is to simply ask, "Just to make sure that I communicated clearly, would you please describe to me your understanding of what we discussed?" It is only when you hear the other person talking in their own words that you can verify that you are both aligned in your understanding.

This simple habit of confirming the other person's understanding can save a lot of time and frustration for everyone involved, and it can help both you and your team members to realize higher levels of performance and fulfillment in your work.

• • • Action Items for Chapter 7 • • •

1. Think of what you expect from your team members in terms of their roles and how they behave while working to achieve the mission, and check to see if you have clearly communicated both the minimum expectations and those of high performers. If not, please schedule time on your calendar to do that now.

2. Create a fifteen-minute calendar event with notifications for reminders, set to repeat once per month to reflect on how often and clearly you're communicating the most important expectations you have for the behavior of team members, and take action as necessary to improve.

3. Reflect on the last couple of projects or tasks you assigned via email or verbally, and see if there are any ways to simplify or better organize the messaging.

4. Look at the next three times on your calendar you know for sure that you'll be assigning a task or project, and write a reminder to yourself to ask the team member to communicate back to you, either via email or verbally, their understanding of the project or task.

8

Improving Well-Being
The Ultimate Win-Win

Growing up in rural Minnesota, Steve Fields learned about the values of hard work and helping others at an early age. The values stuck with him during his college years at Mankato State University (now Minnesota State University). He worked nights and weekends for four years while he earned his undergraduate degree.

After graduating from college, Steve started working on his law degree at the William Mitchell College of Law in St. Paul, Minnesota, in 1995. While attending law school, he also worked full-time as a law clerk at a personal injury law firm.

This was highly unusual at the time. Most law schools expected their students to be focused as much as possible on their degrees.

Working full-time during law school definitely affected Steve's studies, and he wasn't the best student in his class. However, he believes that the experience he gained working directly with clients was much more valuable. He believes that in law, like any other business industry, people skills are more important than technical skills, assuming one has the basic level of competence needed to do a given job.

After graduating from law school, Steve continued working at the personal injury firm as a junior attorney before leaving to start his own firm, Fields Law Firm, in 2001. He started with almost no capital, and worked out of an office in the basement of a warehouse building.

At first, the firm consisted of only Steve and a paralegal. Steve worked almost nonstop, performing nearly all functions of the business. His days would often end by falling asleep at his computer while trying to finish up one last project. As a result of his extremely hard work ethic and an innovative strategy for growing a law firm, it wasn't long before Steve Fields had created a multimillion-dollar, cash-flowing business.

For the most part, Steve isn't interested in accumulating wealth or buying toys, so he reinvested the cash he was accumulating into his law firm. He was able to hire an attorney, then another, and his firm continued to grow in practice areas that help people in need—like those who need disability benefits—and that provide stable and scalable long-term profits for the firm.

However, even as Steve grew his team, he still worked almost nonstop. Most of his work ethic was motivated by helping his clients and employees. But part of it was motivated by a strong, persistent fear of failing and losing everything. Steve sometimes wonders if this fear is somehow related to his first experiences in life when, after he was born, he was separated from his mother and spent time in foster care before being adopted by the people who became his parents.

In 2010, Steve got married. His wife was an attorney at the time, who worked just as much as he did, so getting married didn't slow down his work pace at all. Both Steve and his wife happily worked practically 24/7.

Something changed, though, when Steve and his wife welcomed their first child in 2011. Steve knew that quality time with his son was just as important as, if not more so than, the work he did leading a law firm that helps people in need. So, his wife retired, and he started to slow down a bit.

Almost immediately, he stopped working in the evenings so he could be present with his family. He hasn't worked evenings since.

As Steve slowed down his pace of work, he noticed that in addition to enjoying his life even more than he had before, he was also just as productive, if not more so. Because his mind was less fatigued, he was better able to think strategically and make decisions that really move the needle. The growth of his firm actually accelerated and, before he knew it, he was running a very profitable midsize business with nearly one hundred employees.

As the firm grew, and the relationships deepened between Steve and employees who had been with the firm for a long time, his motivation for growing the firm changed, too. The fear of losing everything gradually dissolved, and he realized he was almost entirely motivated by love.

Steve deeply cares about the well-being of his employees. He wants them to be as happy and successful as possible. He soon realized that the more motivated by love he became, the more joy he found in his work.

In 2018, Steve spent more time reflecting on the benefits of having a healthier balance between work life and time away from work. It became clear to him that he was more successful, both in terms of financial metrics and making a positive impact in the lives of his clients and employees, and that his success would be more sustainable.

And, of course, Steve was happier. He was experiencing more peace of mind and fulfillment.

Reflecting on the benefits to both him and his business made Steve wonder what would happen if he could help the employees at his law firm have more time away from work. Steve and the partner he now had at the firm, Zach Schmoll, started researching the possibility of allowing employees, including attorneys, to work a four-day, thirty-six-hour workweek.

Any attorney reading this is likely laughing out loud and thinking that this is an utterly ridiculous idea. Law firms are notorious for requiring people to work a tremendous number of hours, especially junior attorneys. Most, if not all, junior attorneys show up to an interview assuming that they'll be working around eighty hours per week.

But as Steve and Zach explored the idea and crunched the numbers, they realized that not only could a four-day workweek be possible for their employees, it might actually result in better business outcomes.

Steve and Zach have always wanted to have a law firm that was the best firm to work for. In addition to truly caring about people and genuinely wanting them to be happy at work, they know that an attractive workplace culture helps draw in talented people, which is a key driver of success.

They also know that people skills and strong relationships are the most important drivers of success in any business—assuming a basic level of competency—and especially in a law firm that is helping people during very challenging times in their lives. They believe that if the employees at Fields Law Firm have better emotional well-being, they are more empowered to effectively serve the firm's clients by better caring for them and positively impacting the clients' emotional well-being. This, they believe, can help separate Fields Law Firm from the competition.

It took about a year to come up with a plan that would allow employees at Fields Law Firm to have a four-day workweek that would not create any disruption in the firm's ability to effectively serve clients, and that would allow for continued growth in terms of impact and profitability.

The plan included hiring additional people, which would be a key part of ensuring excellent service for clients. However, even with the added expense of additional employees, Steve and Zach calculated that the four-day workweek would result in improved impact and profitability over the long term. In the spring of 2021, Steve and Zach announced to the firm that they would begin the new four-day workweek in the summer.

Every indication is that it was well worth the time to create this plan, and that Steve and Zach have made a great decision.

Six months after starting the four-day workweek, voluntary turnover at the firm fell from over 54 percent to less than 9 percent, resulting in an annual reduction in expenses related to turnover of more than $2.4 million. It's not very often that a business can reduce an expense by $2.4 million while also making a positive impact on the well-being of employees.

As of this writing, almost two years have passed since Fields Law Firm launched the four-day workweek, and the firm has shown no signs of any negative business impact. In fact, over the last two years, Fields Law Firm has grown even faster—in terms of top-line revenue, number of employees, and profitability—than it had before starting the four-day workweek.

In addition to the positive impacts the four-day workweek has had on business results, there have been incredible impacts on the well-being of employees at the firm. I sent out a survey to employees at Fields Law Firm, and over 96 percent of those who responded stated that "the four-day workweek has had a very positive impact" on their lives.

The survey also provided employees the opportunity to share comments about the four-day workweek, and the impact it has made. Some people shared about how they were able to finally start a new hobby or two that they never had time for in the past. Many people shared how much their stress was reduced because they were able to make doctor appointments and run errands on their off day, instead of having to take time off or get behind on work.

A couple people even shared how, in addition to seeing improvements in their mental health, they have become more productive. They stated they have more energy to give at work because they're more refreshed after a three-day weekend, or because they can use their off day to do some deep work that's hard to squeeze in when they are "at their desks" and expected to be available for meetings and customer interactions.

Others said the impact has been so profound that they could never go back to a five-day workweek. They may become lifelong employees at Fields Law Firm.

A number of employees who are parents shared how the extra day to be with family and take care of household chores has been extremely impactful for them. One team member said the extra time has been literally "life-changing."

A single mother of a young child was particularly touched by the gift of the four-day workweek. This gift has given her fifty extra precious days with her child each year, without having to reduce her income at all. What is the value of having fifty extra days per year with a young child during the formative years when children most want and need to be with a parent? The only answer that comes to my mind is, *this is priceless.*

Work Shouldn't Make People Sick

Of all the universal needs people have for thriving at work, well-being is, without a doubt, the most obvious. If work has a negative impact on a person's well-being, it is clearly not helping that person to thrive, and it is not a sustainable way to drive high performance. Despite being so obvious, well-being is among the universal needs that organizations are consistently failing to meet.

In 2019, the United Nations published a report by the International Labour Organization. The researchers who published the report determined that 36 percent of global workers are working excessively long hours. They also determined that nearly three million people die each year around the world due to disease related to working too much.

Jeffrey Pfeffer, a professor of organizational behavior at the Stanford Graduate School of Business, and author of *Dying for a Paycheck*, believes that at least one hundred thousand Americans die each year from adverse workplace conditions, and that many more become sick, not due to accidents, but because of stress. Pfeffer's research has led him to believe that, at the time he published his book in 2018, "workplace management" *is the fifth leading cause of death in the United States.*

As sad as this situation is, it represents a huge opportunity for you and your team or organization. If you can create a workplace culture that doesn't have a negative impact on the well-being of employees, you will have a significant competitive advantage in terms of both attracting and retaining talented team members and sustaining high levels of performance. And, of course, you'll feel much better about the impact you're making on the lives of employees at your organization.

However, aiming to create a workplace culture that doesn't make people sick is a low bar to aim for. We should be aiming to create workplace cultures that make a positive impact on the well-being of employees. Imagine what our world would be like if going to work actually made people healthier!

This is what we strive for in the companies I've founded. Our highest priority is to ensure that working with us has a positive impact on both the well-being and growth of team members. And I'm confident that if you follow the approach outlined in this book and consistently meet the fourteen universal needs people have for thriving at work, you and your organization will have a positive impact on the well-being of team members, too.

In this chapter, though, we'll focus on the lowest-hanging fruit for improving well-being, which is simply helping team members to work fewer hours.

Reward Results, Not Activity

Many leaders are very reluctant to embrace an idea like helping team members work fewer hours. In many people's minds, there is an assumption that more hours worked equals more productivity. But this is almost certainly a false assumption.

Speaking from my own experience, I interact with people who often talk about how "crazy busy" they are. These people tend to be the least productive people I know.

They engage in lots of activities, but don't produce a lot of value. Most of their activities are those that seem urgent, but aren't really that important. They are constantly reacting to situations and "putting out fires." As a result, they lack the energy and clarity of thought to develop highly leveraged strategies that really move the needle.

Conversely, some of the most productive people I know don't appear to be busy at all. They make time for developing winning strategies and plans, creating long-term assets, and building successful teams to execute their strategies.

For example, Warren Buffett is known for doing very little. He has spent most of his time throughout his career reading and thinking. But when he does act, he produces huge results. By Western standards, he is one of the most productive people of all time. As of this writing, his company, Berkshire Hathaway, is worth $685 billion, the sixth most valuable company in the world.

There's also a large body of research suggesting that working long hours is not only bad for well-being, but it doesn't increase productivity. For instance, Erin Reid, a professor at Boston University's Questrom School of Business, found in her research that managers could not tell the difference between employees who actually worked eighty hours a week and those who just pretended to. She was not able to find any evidence that the employees who worked less accomplished less, or any sign that the employees who worked long hours actually accomplished more.

And a number of studies by Marianna Virtanen and her colleagues at the Finnish Institute of Occupational Health suggest that overworking can have a negative impact on financial results. They have found that overwork is correlated with higher absenteeism, increased turnover, and increased health insurance costs.

The problem with assuming that more hours worked equals more productivity is that it creates a workplace culture that rewards activity instead of results. Employees in cultures like this think that the way to get ahead is to look very busy. So, they do lots of "stuff." Or at least appear to.

This creates a vicious cycle. Everyone works long hours, trying to do as much "stuff" as they can. But this creates a lot of stress, which quickly burns people out, and leads to bad decisions and the erosion of relationships. And it's hard for these employees to make an impact because they're spending most of their time on tasks that are urgent but not important. This accelerates burnout because people don't find much meaning in their work, which is a universal need for thriving at work.

A better approach is to create a culture in which everyone is less concerned with activity, and more concerned with achieving results and making an impact. Some essential steps for creating this type of culture include ensuring that there is a clear strategy for the team or organization, that the strategy is aligned with measurable impacts on achieving the mission, and that employees' goals are aligned with the strategic goals.

For teams and organizations that lack the clarity and alignment described in the previous paragraph, it can take some time to attain that clarity and alignment. To take action immediately toward improving the impact your workplace culture makes on the well-being of employees, you could start with the simple habit of encouraging people to work fewer hours.

Two Simple Habits for Improving Well-Being and Performance

Because the well-being of our employees is the top priority at the companies I've founded, we offer a thirty-two-hour workweek. We offer competitive forty-hour-per-week salaries, but we strongly encourage employees to only spend thirty-two hours per week performing work that's in their job descriptions. We ask that they spend an average of two hours per week engaged in self-directed learning, and two hours per week volunteering their time to serve the community in a way that allows them to do something they enjoy, that they're good at, and to see the impact they're making as quickly as possible.

Just as Steve Fields and other leaders who have adopted some variation of a four-day workweek have discovered, we've found zero evidence that we're losing any productivity over the long term with this approach. In fact, there is evidence to suggest that we're more efficient and more productive with this approach. And it certainly helps with attracting and retaining talented people who are great culture fits.

That being said, a four-day workweek may not be right for your team or organization right now. It may never be right for your organization. And it takes a good deal of planning and effort for an organization to transition to a four-day workweek.

However, any leader can immediately begin having a positive impact on the well-being of employees by encouraging team members to work no more than forty hours per week as the norm (there may be short-term exceptions for big opportunities that require extra time), and creating clear expectations around work-related communication when employees are away from their desks.

A simple first step is to let employees know that working more than forty hours per week as the norm will not help them advance their careers. You could go a step further and let team members know that working more than forty hours a week is seen as a negative trait. Of course, if you're part of a team or organization that has historically rewarded people who work long hours, you may have to provide a good deal of context when you set the new expectation.

The first habit for helping to improve the well-being of team members is to have regular coaching meetings to help people be more efficient. These meetings can occur during your regular one-to-one meetings with team members. They could also just be informal meetings that happen spontaneously when you notice employees working too many hours.

For instance, Steve Fields and Zach Schmoll at Fields Law Firm genuinely want people to work no more than thirty-six hours per week so employees can have more quality time away from work doing whatever is important to them. So they have made it a habit to have a coaching conversation whenever they notice someone working too many hours.

They'll jokingly ask a question like, "What's going on? Why are you working so long today?"

Often, when the employee explains why they worked so long, Steve or Zach discover that the employee is simply being inefficient, due to a lack of experience in a newer area. Steve or Zach take some time right then, or very soon thereafter, to coach the employee on ways to be more efficient, explaining that the motivation is to help them spend less time at work.

The second habit is to do the best you can to eliminate the expectation that employees should be responding to non-urgent work-related communication when they're away from their desks. This is particularly important for team members who are virtual because the boundaries between work time and personal time have almost vanished for them.

The approach that you would use to execute on this idea will vary depending on the position of the team members. Let's start with team members who aren't customer facing or managers.

First, I recommend you establish or reinforce that they are not expected to check or reply to work-related emails or chat messages when they're away from their desks. You could even frame this new expectation by saying that you want to do better at having a positive impact on the well-being of team members.

Second, do your best to refrain from calling or texting team members when they're not working, unless it's a true emergency, and encourage team members to do the same for each other.

Of course, some team members are customer facing or need to check work-related communication when they're away from their desks for some other reason. In some cases, having an on-call rotation might help ensure that people can unplug when they're away from their desks and not on call. In other cases, an on-call rotation may not be practical, and certain team members may need to check email or chat when they're away from their desks.

If that's the case, you could encourage team members to simply shut off email and chat notifications so they don't feel like they need to be constantly checking their phones. Instead, you could encourage them to set up a regular cadence for checking for emails or chat messages. For some people, checking once or twice per day to see if there's anything urgent to attend to might be enough. For others, it might have to be once every two hours or so.

What's most important is to develop a habit of frequently communicating to team members that their well-being is very important to you and that you want to keep open lines of communication about ensuring that they're happy with their ability to enjoy their time away from work and recharge. This can be done during regular one-to-one meetings.

If you make a habit of having these types of conversations, the natural side effect will be that you help team members refrain from working more than forty hours per week and eliminate the perception that employees need to constantly check their emails and phones for work-related communications when they're not at their desks.

These two simple habits can help your team or organization dramatically improve performance by helping to shift the focus from measuring activity to measuring results while simultaneously helping you to improve the mental and physical health of your employees. And it will help you and other leaders in your organization to realize more joy and fulfillment at work.

• • • Action Items for Chapter 8 • • •

1. Create a sixty-minute calendar event set to repeat each quarter to take time to get clarity on the strategic goals for the quarter and help any leaders who report to you do the same. Then, leaders should clearly communicate those goals to team members and work with team members to establish key performance indicators (KPIs) to help them know if they're on track.

2. Create a calendar event with a pop-up notification that reminds you to keep an eye out for team members who are looking busy or working too many hours and help them find ways to be more efficient so that they can achieve their goals without burning themselves out.

3. Take a few minutes right now, per the guidance in this chapter, to write a plan for how you're going to set or reinforce the expectations around work-related communication while employees are away from their desks.

4. Add a note to your agenda for one or two one-to-one meetings per quarter to ask about how work is affecting the well-being of your team members and to see if there's any way you can better help them thrive at work, or away from work. I recommend not discussing work performance at all during this meeting.

9

Giving People the Tools
They Need to Succeed

A Simple, High-Yield Investment

Lieutenant Colonel (LTC) Julio Acosta was preparing for a long day. As the battalion commander, his duties included many tasks that he loved. But much of this day would be spent conducting non-judicial punishment (NJP), which he loathed.

In the US Army, as in other branches of the military, commanders have the power to use NJP to punish soldiers who have broken a law or military rule without sending the soldier to a court-martial, which is the equivalent of a trial that can result in a felony conviction.

LTC Acosta was going through the files for each of the soldiers that he would be seeing at NJP that day, one of the many aspects of the NJP process he despised. It always saddened him to read of young soldiers who made mistakes that could seriously hinder their careers in the Army. But one of the files offered him a glimmer of hope for the day.

One of the soldiers he would be seeing was a young private first class (PFC) who we'll call Tammy Jackson. Until recently, PFC Jackson had apparently been a model soldier. But after having her baby and returning from parental leave, she started showing up late twice each week for the 6:30 AM morning formation, which is a mandatory morning meeting that happens every workday.

In the file, LTC Acosta noticed that her leaders had reprimanded her numerous times for being late. Her leaders also noted how her attitude declined very sharply after the first reprimand. Despite repeated reprimands, she still didn't arrive at the morning formation on time on Tuesdays and Fridays, and her attitude continued to decline.

Later that day, when PFC Jackson stepped into the office where LTC Acosta was holding NJP, she looked both frustrated and sad. LTC Acosta didn't open her file, as he normally would. Instead, he simply looked at her and said, "PFC Jackson, it seems that something has changed for you since returning from parental leave. Please tell me what's going on."

PFC Jackson replied, "Sir, as you know, I recently had a baby."

"Yes. I am aware of this," replied LTC Acosta.

"But," PFC Jackson continued, "you probably don't know that her father left me when he found out I was pregnant, so I'm a single mom now."

"I did not know that," LTC Acosta said.

"Fortunately, my mom lives near the base. And, three days each week, she can take care of my baby," PFC Jackson said.

LTC Acosta listened intently, with compassion, and nodded for her to keep going.

"But, on Tuesdays and Fridays, my mom has to work in the morning, and she can't watch the baby. So I have to use the daycare on base."

LTC Acosta remembered that Tuesdays and Fridays were the days PFC Jackson was late.

"Okay. Please continue," he said.

"Sir, the daycare on base doesn't open until 6:30 AM," she said.

LTC Acosta immediately filled in the space: "And morning formation is at 6:30 AM. Did you tell your sergeant about this?"

"Yes, sir. I did. He said, 'That's the way it is,' and that I need to figure something out to make sure I show up at formation time," she replied.

"PFC Jackson, please report back to duty. I'm going to take care of this, and I'll have a word with your sergeant, too."

PFC Jackson immediately stood up a little straighter, and appeared visibly relieved. "Yes, sir," she replied.

LTC Acosta knew that this was an issue that could be affecting a number of soldiers, not just PFC Jackson. So he immediately got on the phone with the base daycare and was able to convince them to open at 6:00 AM, starting the following week. He then got on the phone and called the office where PFC Jackson worked, asked to speak to her, and informed her of the change.

PFC Jackson's attitude improved immediately. In fact, she became one of the most enthusiastic soldiers in the unit. She went on to become a star performer, she was promoted ahead of schedule, and was regarded by her leaders as one of the most valuable members of the unit.

People Usually Aren't the Problem

Of all the universal needs people have for thriving at work and being fully engaged, having what we need to do our jobs well is probably most tightly correlated with the absence of anxiety and frustration, according to the Gallup organization. However, research from Gallup has also found that, globally, only about one out of three employees strongly agree that they have what they need to do their job *correctly*, let alone at a high level.

Taking the time to ask team members what they need to do their jobs well, and what obstacles might be in their way, is a critical component of realizing high levels of performance. Perhaps more importantly, this is a simple yet powerful way to demonstrate to team members that you truly care about them and are committed to helping them not only succeed, but thrive.

When team members aren't meeting expectations, I strongly encourage you to not immediately assume that the problem is with the team member. It's quite possible that you didn't communicate an expectation clearly. If you verify with a team member that expectations are clear, the next place to look is the system in which the team member is working.

W. Edwards Deming, the late researcher known as "the Father of Quality," suggested that, according to his research and experience, roughly 90 percent of performance gaps are caused by processes, and only 10 percent are caused by people. This is why it is essential to regularly ask team members about what they need to do great work, and what could be getting in the way.

We should be asking these questions every month, whether or not there are performance gaps. If there are gaps, this could very likely be the cause. And, even if there aren't gaps, asking these questions can help prevent future gaps, and improve performance even further.

Asking team members these questions is best done during one-to-one meetings so you can have some back-and-forth and get to the root cause of potential issues. Whenever a lack of resources or an obstacle is mentioned, I recommend asking at least a couple of follow-up questions, which could be as simple as, "Would you please tell me more about that?"

Once you've heard about the issue in depth, I recommend asking the team member what they suggest for resolving it. Then, based on the information you've gathered, you can decide what is the best course of action.

If it's something you can easily resolve, it might be best for you to resolve the issue on your own. For instance, LTC Acosta knew that he could likely work with the officer in charge of the base daycare to get the hours changed. He didn't need the help of his commanding officer.

If it's an issue that senior management could easily resolve, you could bring it to their attention and ask for their help. The sergeant who was PFC Jackson's direct supervisor would not have been able to contact the officer in charge of the daycare directly and ask him to consider changing their hours.

However, if his top priority had been the success of the soldiers that reported to him, he would have brought this issue up the chain of command until he reached the commanding general of the base, if needed. As it turns out, it wouldn't have needed to go that far. His battalion commander, LTC Acosta, was willing and able to resolve the issue.

It's important to note here that, if leaders have a habit of sending signals that they don't want to hear about problems or "bad news," your organization will likely run into issues similar to what LTC Acosta encountered. Somewhere in the chain of command, there was likely a leader who indicated that he didn't want to hear about soldiers' personal issues, or he wasn't going to work to raise an issue like that up the chain of command.

As a result, the sergeant who supervised PFC Jackson probably didn't think there was any chance of solving a high-level problem like the hours for the daycare on base. So, he didn't even try. He just told PFC Jackson, "That's the way it is. You figure it out."

Some issues aren't so simple to solve. They are the result of complex processes that individuals and teams apply in their daily work. For complex issues with work-related processes, it is often best for the individual or team to come up with a solution for improving the process in question.

Whenever possible, I recommend giving the team ownership of improving the process. You could help them come up with small experiments and the associated metrics to measure the impact of the changes, so they can gradually either prove or disprove their hypothesis. You could also let them know that if they need any help removing roadblocks in the form of bureaucracy or other departments, you'll be happy to do what you can to help remove them.

This approach is a powerful way to create leverage in your team or organization. It's easy to assume that if a team is not hitting goals, the answer is to ask people to work more hours, or to apply more resources, like hiring more people. But that does not create leverage. A team has to commit those resources forever to continue hitting the goals.

The better solution is to improve the processes that are involved in hitting goals. Once you've invested the resources to improve the process, you no longer need to invest further resources. This creates leverage, as well as a much better return on investment.

If you can develop the habit of asking people what they need to do their best work, and what obstacles could be getting in their way, you'll likely uncover a number of processes that could be improved. I'm confident that you'll see significant decreases in frustration and its results, namely low engagement and high turnover. In the absence of this frustration, you'll notice higher levels of engagement and performance, and you'll be better able to retain your best team members.

• • • Action Item for Chapter 9 • • •

Put a reminder on your calendar to check in with team members every month to ask what additional resources they might need to thrive and do their best work, and to check in regarding any obstacles that might be preventing team members from thriving. Then commit to doing whatever you can to help them get what they need, remove the obstacles, and/or empower team members to improve the processes with which they're involved.

10

Leveraging Strengths

How to Unlock Untapped Energy

Ricky, as he was known growing up, was doing terribly in school. At eight years old, he still couldn't read. This was largely due to the fact that he couldn't make out the letters on the chalkboard. Even though he sat in the front of his classroom, the words and numbers were a blur.

Ricky eventually had his eyes tested. It was determined that he was nearsighted. Nevertheless, even after getting glasses, the letters and numbers on the board appeared all jumbled. They just didn't make sense. Ricky would later learn that he has dyslexia.

Unfortunately, Ricky was in his first year at a boarding school near London, England, in the 1950s. Very few people had heard of dyslexia at that point. This meant that people assumed Ricky was lazy or stupid, or both. In those days, at boarding schools in England, children were spanked for being lazy or stupid. For a while, Ricky was spanked once or twice every week.

His misery ended, though, when people learned how good he was at sports. He soon became the captain of three different sports teams.

In England, that meant that he was essentially a superhero. All the kids loved him and the school staff gradually let up on the spankings.

Everything was going so well for Ricky that he didn't even care that he couldn't read or write. All that changed, though, when he severely injured his knee during a rugby match. He was no longer able to play sports because his knee would buckle whenever he tried to run.

The spankings began once again. In fact, because Ricky was doing so poorly in school and no longer had the protection of being a star athlete, the spankings became even more frequent. But trying to learn at school was so frustrating for him that he grew to prefer the beatings.

Ricky eventually discovered that he actually loved learning, as long as it was tied to practical, real-life activities. He particularly loved learning about how to start and run businesses, especially using math to predict whether or not a business would be profitable.

Fortunately for Ricky, his mother was an entrepreneur who sparked his interest in business at an early age. As a young teen, Ricky tried to start a Christmas tree business. According to his calculations, it should have been very profitable. But he didn't account for rabbits eating the saplings as they sprouted, so his Christmas tree business ended after the first attempt at growing trees.

Undeterred, Ricky then started a business selling birds called budgies. After calculating how fast the birds breed, how much it costs to feed them, and the potential year-round demand, Ricky was very excited about the potential for profit. He even convinced his father to help him build an aviary.

It turned out that Ricky had significantly overestimated the demand for budgies in his area. To his surprise, not everyone in town wanted more than two budgies. The budgie business failed, too.

Ricky didn't mind these setbacks at all, though. In fact, he viewed each business that didn't work not as a failure, but as an opportunity to learn and increase the chances of success in the future. Indeed, he had success with his next venture. Ricky and his partner, Jonny, started a magazine, called *Student*, which would give students across England a voice and a platform for change.

Ricky was better able to calculate potential profit margins and market sizes. He determined that if they targeted high school students, the market would be too small, since university students probably wouldn't be interested in reading a magazine for high schoolers. Instead, they decided to focus on university students as their target market, since high school students would definitely want to read something targeted to university students.

Ricky was very excited about this project. There were so many fun problems to solve. He would continue learning about math and writing in a way that he loved.

He was so excited, he overcame any and all fear of rejection and cold-called large companies, like National Westminster Bank and Coca-Cola, as a fifteen-year-old boy. And when cold-calling didn't work, he wrote hundreds of letters to potential advertisers.

After a year of hard work, Ricky finally started to see some success. His team at *Student* was able to land their first advertiser, and the famed cartoonist Gerald Scarfe agreed to be interviewed by the magazine and submit a cartoon. Ricky's dream of creating a magazine was finally becoming a reality.

But school was going worse than ever. Ricky continued to fail exams and, one by one, he quit going to classes. By the time he was sixteen, he had quit going to all of his classes except for ancient history. Before he turned seventeen, Ricky left school altogether. When he left, the headmaster of the school said, "I predict that you will either go to prison or become a millionaire."

Had Ricky tried to force himself to continue to work hard in an area where he was so weak—at school—the headmaster may very well have been right about Ricky going to prison. He might have struggled to get a job that didn't pay much, wasn't fulfilling, and frustrated him to the point that he would become addicted to drugs and/or crime. The headmaster did turn out to be *almost* right with his prediction.

The first issue of *Student* was published in 1968. Before long, the magazine achieved a modicum of success. When the staff of *Student* reached about twenty, Ricky had an idea for a business that seemed like it would be just as fun as a magazine: a record distribution company.

Ricky has always been more interested in having fun and making an impact than he has been in making money. So, in 1972, he founded a discount record shop that would eventually become one of the most successful record labels in the world, signing some of the biggest names in music, including the Rolling Stones, U2, Paula Abdul, Janet Jackson, and Coldplay.

When the company was founded, though, there was no one on the team who knew much about running a real business. They considered themselves "virgins" in business. This inspired the team to name the company Virgin Records.

Ricky is better known today as Richard Branson. He is one of the most successful businesspeople in history, by every metric. He is not a millionaire, but a billionaire. He has successfully entered and disrupted a range of industries, including the airline, cola, train, mobile phone, cruise ship, and hotel industries. And his companies are known for being among the best places in the world to work.

The Power of Helping People Leverage Their Strengths

Please take a moment to remember a time when you were so engaged in an activity that time seemed to disappear, or passed extremely fast, perhaps while playing a sport, or creating art, or working on a challenging project at work. Do you remember what it felt like to be "in the zone"?

Being "in the zone" is one of the most enjoyable experiences people can have. In the 1970s, researchers in positive psychology became interested in this state, which they began calling "flow state." Flow state is associated with increased happiness, higher intrinsic motivation, greater creativity, and better emotional regulation. It's also associated with incredible levels of productivity.

Clearly, as leaders, it would be well worth our effort to help team members spend more time in flow state. Since flow state occurs when we are faced with a challenging task that we believe we have the skills to accomplish, a simple way for managers to help team members spend more time in flow state is to help them spend more time working on challenging projects that leverage what team members are naturally best at.

According to research from the Gallup organization, only one in three employees strongly agree that they have the opportunity to do what they do best every day. And, by doubling that ratio, organizations could realize a 6 percent increase in customer engagement scores, an 11 percent increase in profitability, a 30 percent reduction in turnover, and a 36 percent reduction in safety incidents.

Gallup also found that engaged employees spend their time with a 4:1 ratio of time doing what they do best versus time doing things that they don't do well. For actively disengaged employees, that ratio was 1:1. This means that we need to do more than just create a balance between performing tasks that are strengths and those that are weaknesses. We need to help team members spend as much time as possible doing what they're best at.

Identifying and Leveraging Strengths

The first step to helping team members spend more time doing what they're best at is to identify their strengths. This can be done with a combination of observing where an individual team member excels, asking the individual what she believes her strengths are, and asking her team members to share what they believe that individual is best at. If you'd like to take this approach to a higher level, you could use a formal assessment, like CliftonStrengths.

Once you've identified some areas where a team member is naturally strong, I recommend spending less time working on fixing weaknesses and more time finding ways to help her do more of what she's naturally good at. A good rule of thumb is to help people get to about average for areas that aren't their strengths, little by little, focusing more time on utilizing and growing strengths. And, once a person is about average in an area that isn't a natural strength, stop spending any energy trying to improve that area so the team member can focus entirely on utilizing and growing strengths.

You can also apply this approach for yourself, as a leader, just as Richard Branson did. He learned at a young age that he wasn't naturally strong at academic learning, which focuses on details. However, he learned that he was very strong at connecting dots that others didn't. He could see the "big picture" very quickly.

Richard has worked to get to about average at reading and other detail-type skills. But he has focused almost entirely on developing inspiring visions and effective strategies. Instead of trying to be good at details himself, he has hired people who are strong with details to build well-rounded leadership teams.

Working to help team members spend more time doing what they're naturally good at could mean making little adjustments over time. Or, in some cases, it could mean moving a team member to a new role where the individual is much more likely to succeed. For most teams, making little adjustments over time is the more realistic approach.

For example, you could reassign some tasks so a task that one individual is not suited for is reassigned to another team member who is better suited for the task. If you're able to remove some tasks that are not ideal for the team member, you could then help her spend more time doing what she's naturally good at. This might mean delegating tasks to the team member that you currently perform, which you'll learn more about in chapter fourteen, or working with the individual to create additional projects that maximize their strengths and add value for the team.

In some cases, these additional projects can turn into a new role for a team member. If a project adds enough value to justify creating a new position to work on it, this can be the ultimate scenario for helping a team member to spend as much time as possible doing what he's best at.

Regardless of the mechanism you choose, by helping team members spend as much time as possible doing what they do best, you'll see dramatic increases in engagement and productivity while also helping your team members enjoy their work more. This will also help you to retain your best employees and attract top talent. And you might just help a team member create a dream job that helps both the team member and your organization to grow.

• • • Action Items for Chapter 10 • • •

1. Write out a plan for how you'll identify the strengths and weaknesses of your team members.

2. Create a new calendar event for some time in the next five days with a notification to remind you to execute on the plan for identifying strengths and weaknesses.

3. Create a thirty-minute calendar event for next week, which repeats once each quarter, in which you spend at least thirty minutes thinking about and acting on ways to help team members do more of what they're best at. (I recommend doing this in one segment so you can get in the zone and move tasks between team members if needed.)

11

Helping People Feel Like Their Ideas Matter

A Simple Way to Improve Both
Engagement and Inclusion

K arin Hurt had spent about a decade in roles related to HR, as well as a three-year stint running customer service call centers with hundreds of employees. Nearly 95 percent of the people who worked in the call centers were women. And, during her time in HR, most of her managers and direct reports were women.

Then, in March 2009, Karin was asked to become the director of retail sales and operations for Verizon Wireless in Washington, Baltimore, and Virginia, a total of 110 stores. Her organization included 2,200 employees, mostly men. And thirteen out of fourteen of her direct reports were men.

In addition to the challenge of being a woman leading a team of almost entirely men, her direct reports, and most of the employees in her organization, had been in sales their entire careers. Karin had never sold anything in her life, except for a few boxes of Girl Scout cookies, and she wasn't even particularly good at that. (For perspective, that is somewhat analogous to struggling to sell water to a person in a burning-hot desert who hasn't had a sip of water for two days.)

Needless to say, when Karin stepped into her new role, many people were wondering, and in some cases expressing, "Why, exactly, are you in charge now?" One district manager stated openly that Karin was unqualified for the job, and that "this was clearly a diversity, succession-planning move."

However, the fact that she would almost certainly face challenges earning the respect of her team was not her biggest concern. Her biggest concern was the lines of people that were standing outside the doors of her 110 retail stores. Normally, of course, this is a good thing. But for Karin, it was very scary.

A new type of phone was released on June 29, 2007. It was grabbing enormous amounts of market share. AT&T won exclusive rights to sell this popular new phone in their retail stores. Verizon could not offer it in theirs.

The lines of people outside of Karin's stores weren't there because of excitement about Verizon Wireless. They were there to find out when their contracts ended so they could transfer to AT&T and get an iPhone.

So Karin had found herself leading a team of mostly men who were career salespeople, despite knowing almost nothing about sales herself, and her team members now felt that they had nothing they could sell. No one wanted what they had to offer. When I spoke with Karin about this, she told me that this was one of the most challenging times of her entire career.

Although Karin knew very little about selling, she had spent enough time in her HR roles interacting with salespeople to know one very important fact. She knew that if salespeople *think* they can't sell, they can't sell. Her team was demoralized. She knew that for her team to succeed, she would have to change their mindsets as quickly as possible.

Karin also knew that at least some of the salespeople on her team must have been successfully selling something. She asked the data analyst on her team to provide her with the list of the top ten salespeople in her organization. Then she went to their stores and began following the successful salespeople around and asking them about what they were doing.

She was particularly intrigued by a salesperson named Yomi. After spending some time with Yomi, she noticed that he was asking a particular question in every single conversation he had with customers: "Where do you work?"

So, Karin asked him, "Yomi, why do you do that? Is that just to build rapport?"

As Karin describes in her book *Courageous Cultures*, Yomi replied, "No, Karin. I ask where they work because I want to know if they own a small business. Those small business owners don't want an iPhone for their businesses—it's so new that businesspeople are worried about data security. They still want the Blackberry or a push-to-talk-phone. When I find out they own a business, I tell them all about our great new small business plans. I'm bringing over five, ten, and twenty lines at a time. My customers are thrilled and they tell their friends to come see me."

Karin immediately set up a meeting with her district managers and said, "Yomi has figured it out. I think he's got the solution to our sales issue."

The district managers all replied with something like, "Oh, Karin, that's just Yomi being Yomi."

"What do you mean?" Karin replied.

They said, "Yomi has been our best salesperson forever. He could sell ice to Eskimos. We've tried the small business thing. It will never work."

Karin knew that she needed to express confident humility in this situation. She told the team that it's certainly possible that this wouldn't work out as a long-term strategy, but it was worth a test. To increase buy-in, she asked for ideas for how to make the test as fun as possible.

The team ended up running a test on the following Tuesday. Every single employee would ask every single customer where they worked. And it would be like a party.

They bought Red Bull for everyone. People dressed up in costumes. There were balloons in the stores. And, before they went out to the sales floor that day, they had meetings that were like pep rallies to get people excited and clarify the expectations.

On that random Tuesday, sales quadrupled. Not just sales of business lines, but total lines sold.

The next day, Karin held an all-hands meeting for every employee working in her region. She confidently said, "If this approach can work on a random Tuesday, it can work any day."

People were excited. They believed that they could sell again. They were confident they had a valuable solution for customers. All thanks to the idea of one employee, named Yomi, and a leader who was open to his ideas and took action on them.

In a short time, business lines grew from 2 percent of total sales to 8 percent. But it seemed to plateau there. So Karin asked her team for more ideas for improving sales.

She made it clear that selling small business lines was the core strategy. But she let each store decide how they could best sell small business lines. Many stores had interesting ideas to pitch.

Karin's Washington, DC, team let her know that in their store most of the customers were lawyers and politicians who would probably respond much better to people in suits than to people in polo shirts. The team asked for a stipend to get suits. Karin approved it.

Karin's team let her know that in their Cedar Bluff, VA, store, which is actually in a log cabin, the clients were mostly farmers and contractors who probably wouldn't respond as well to someone in a suit, but they really care about their businesses and want to be treated as professionals.

The Cedar Bluff store asked to make changes to the building and convert an upstairs loft into a small business center where customers could have a snack, get work done, and be treated with deep respect for their businesses. Karin approved it. The store became the top-selling small business line store in the region.

By the time Karin was promoted out of her position, her team was leading the nation and won the President's Award for customer growth. Her once-demoralized team was now a team of energized winners.

The Power of Contributing Ideas

A core need we all share as humans is to feel as though we're contributing in ways that add value for others. One could make a good argument that this is the primary factor for determining whether or not we find our lives meaningful and fulfilling. Feeling as though we're contributing at work is a key factor of realizing meaning in our jobs, which is a universal need people have for thriving in the workplace (you'll learn more about this in chapter eighteen).

One of the easiest ways to contribute is to share helpful ideas for improving the way things are done. A great idea can occur in an instant, and it can be shared almost as fast. And, of course, one great idea could add massive value for customers, a team, an organization, or even society.

Yomi's simple idea regarding asking customers where they work added extraordinary value for Karin Hurt's team at Verizon. It's possible that his idea saved Verizon from experiencing catastrophic consequences. And, Karin's habit of asking for ideas from team members helped her team to make the most out of Yomi's initial idea.

Encouraging team members to share ideas they have is a highly leveraged activity for leaders. And it's an essential one.

As a result of a variety of factors, change is happening faster and faster every year. From now on, teams and organizations must be very agile—able to quickly adapt to change—to thrive, or even survive, in some cases. A key element of agility is ensuring that everyone in a team or organization is thinking about how to continuously improve the way things are done.

If managers, or worse, executives, are the only ones thinking about how to improve, or respond to change, many of the best ideas will be missed. This is because individual contributors have the most interactions with end users of products and services. They have access to insights that managers and executives usually do not. Thus, creating the conditions for team members to more frequently share ideas meets important needs for both the team members and the organization.

Helping People Feel Like Their Ideas Matter

There are two basic steps to building a culture in which team members regularly share their ideas. First, leaders at all levels need to cultivate the habit of asking team members for their ideas whenever they are trying to solve a problem or improve something. This means regularly asking team members questions like the following:

- "What are your thoughts about how to do this?"
- "What would you do if you were me?"
- "How do you think we could do this better?"

If you ask questions like these in group brainstorming sessions, it's very important that the leader speak last, and hold off on sharing their ideas until team members have shared theirs. As soon as the leader shares an idea, it can constrain how others think because of a subconscious bias to want to "please the leader."

The second step to building a culture in which team members regularly share their ideas is to positively reinforce the behavior you want to see. Most importantly, this means making sure people feel safe to share their ideas, even if those ideas are critical of management. Great leaders not only welcome dissenting ideas; they actively encourage them.

One way to actively encourage ideas that are dissenting or critical of leadership is to publicly praise or even reward people who share those types of ideas. Every time team members see someone being praised for sharing such ideas, they'll feel safer to do the same. This is one of the most powerful ways to help a team or organization avoid serious failures, and achieve the highest levels of success.

It's also essential to ensure that people feel heard when they share ideas. This doesn't mean you need to act on every idea that is shared. It just means that you need to acknowledge every idea that is shared.

We need to thank team members for every idea they offer up. If we decide not to act on an idea that is shared, we should explain why. Taking the time to explain why an idea doesn't fit in with the current strategic plan, or with our values, ensures the team member feels heard, which is a critical element of feeling like one's opinion matters.

According to a global study conducted by the Workforce Institute at UKG and Workplace Intelligence, ensuring team members feel heard is highly correlated with business success. The researchers found that highly engaged employees are *three times* more likely to say they feel heard at their workplace (92 percent) than highly disengaged employees (just 30 percent). The researchers also found that 74 percent of employees report they are more effective at their job when they feel heard, and 88 percent of employees whose companies financially outperform others in their industry feel heard compared to 62 percent of employees at financially underperforming companies.

Taking the time to explain why an idea doesn't fit in with the current strategic plan, or with your values, also helps team members offer better ideas going forward. Thus, this is an extremely highly leveraged activity.

When some leaders first consider the practice of soliciting ideas from team members, they get concerned that they may become overwhelmed with the volume of ideas. In the short term, it may be challenging to respond to every idea and explain why certain ideas aren't acted upon. However, every time you do, you're helping your team members to better understand the values and strategic objectives of the team or organization.

Over time, this will reduce the number of ideas you receive because you'll only be receiving ideas that are aligned with the values and strategic goals. More importantly, the ideas you receive will get better and better. Receiving game-changing ideas from team members may become the norm.

When an idea is aligned with the current strategy and your values, leaders should try to act as often as possible. This could mean taking action yourself or delegating the execution to team members. And, just as with critical or dissenting ideas, leaders should publicly recognize and appreciate the person who shared the idea to help encourage similar efforts from other team members going forward.

The Secret to Building and Maintaining Diversity

Most leaders are aware of the benefits of having diverse teams. Diverse teams have been shown to be more creative and more likely to innovate. They are also more likely to help organizations capture new markets.

One critical element of having diverse teams is to intentionally seek out diverse candidates in the hiring process so the organization is more likely to find a new hire who is not only the best fit for the job, but also somehow diverse from the average employee. However, this approach will fail without ensuring that equity and inclusion are practiced by leaders. This is why people ops professionals don't launch "diversity" initiatives. They launch "diversity, equity, and inclusion" (DEI) initiatives.

A key to ensuring that talented team members of diverse backgrounds stay at an organization, and thereby make it easier to attract and retain more talented team members of diverse backgrounds, is to ensure that team members feel heard. If team members of diverse backgrounds share ideas and don't feel heard, they will likely feel as though the team or organization is not equitable or inclusive.

Conversely, by simply taking the time to acknowledge and appreciate ideas shared by all team members, and let them know why certain ideas aren't acted on, people feel like their opinions matter. They feel heard. They feel included and important. Isn't this how everyone wants to feel?

• • • Action Items for Chapter 11 • • •

1. Create a weekly calendar reminder for the next thirty days to take five to ten minutes to think about problems you're trying to solve, or areas you're trying to improve, and ask your team members for their ideas.

2. Update meeting notes or calendar events for any group meetings you have with team members for the next thirty days to remind you to review your plan for asking team members about their ideas before you share yours.

3. Create a new, ten-minute calendar event with a reminder for one day each week for the next four weeks to remind you to reflect on any ideas that have been shared by team members—and to thank the team members who shared the ideas—then either act on them, delegate action on them, or explain why those ideas won't be acted on now.

12

Providing Feedback That
Inspires Greatness

How to Transform Judgment into Inspiration

Everyone had high expectations for Jadon Williams. Some people thought he might become the next superstar quarterback in the National Football League (NFL).

He was the perfect height at 6'5" tall. He was lightning fast, running the 40-yard dash in just under 4.25 seconds. He had one of the strongest arms NFL recruiters had ever seen. And, he seemed to be able to pick defenses apart with the skilled precision of a surgeon.

The preseason had gone very well for Williams. He had been running well and passing even better, leading the team to an undefeated record.

The first game of the regular season, however, did not go well. Although his running game was solid, Williams threw three interceptions, and the team lost. For some reason, though—perhaps wanting to avoid difficult conversations or not disrupt his mindset—no one gave Williams any feedback on his performance after the game.

The second game of the season was just as bad. Williams threw two interceptions, and he only completed 35 percent of his pass attempts. Still, no one gave him any feedback to help him improve.

The whole season went on like this. Williams averaged 2.8 interceptions per game, only one touchdown per game, and had a completion percentage of 37 percent. It wasn't until after the last game of the year that the head coach finally sat Williams down and gave him feedback.

He said, "Jadon, as I'm sure you're aware, you've had a terrible season. We're going to have to let you go. Oh, by the way, your elbow is flaring out too much when you throw, and that's probably why you keep throwing the ball so poorly, with so many interceptions."

· · · · · ·

Unlike the rest of the stories in this book, the one above never happened, and is meant to be a parody. However, it probably failed as a parody because only those unfamiliar with professional sports would believe that Jadon Williams wasn't given feedback within minutes of throwing his first interception, much less the rest of the season.

Anyone even moderately familiar with professional sports would realize that the story above is utterly ridiculous, and it would never, ever happen. Sadly, though, stories like the one above are happening every single year in organizations all over the world.

As discussed in greater detail in chapter fourteen, a universal need that people have at work, and in life in general, is to grow. Somewhere inside each one of us is a drive to be a little bit better today than we were yesterday.

People with a high achievement drive know that feedback is a key to growing, so they actively seek it out. Consider the best athletes in the world. They all have multiple coaches giving them almost continuous feedback. A quarterback in the NFL probably gets feedback, if needed, within minutes or even seconds.

This is one of the primary reasons I created the approach outlined in Part 1. It's hard for managers to get the feedback from direct reports that we need to grow and more consistently be the leaders we aspire to be. Thus, an anonymous, easy-to-use feedback system is very helpful for leaders.

Although most managers are high achievers who crave feedback to help them grow, we often forget that everyone on our team has this need, too. As a result, feedback often isn't provided to team members with nearly enough frequency.

Studies suggest that 60 to 70 percent of employees say they don't receive feedback often enough. In some cases, team members don't get any feedback until an annual review. But feedback at an annual review shouldn't be new. There should be no surprises.

If we wait until an annual or bi-annual review to give feedback, the feedback isn't about coaching someone to be their best. It's about judgment. This is not helpful. In fact, this type of feedback can actually reduce engagement and lead to worsened performance.

There are a variety of reasons why managers fail to provide feedback frequently enough. One reason is that they've never been trained on the importance of feedback. Another reason is that they're very busy, and this just seems like one more thing they need to do. Another reason is that sometimes feedback conversations are uncomfortable, and people tend to avoid things that make them uncomfortable.

Here's what I recommend to overcome these very valid obstacles.

Remember, to be a highly effective leader who also realizes deep meaning in your work, it is essential to see your primary job as inspiring greatness in your team members by serving as a coach who helps people thrive (to be happy, great human beings who do great work). The more you embody this approach to leadership, the less uncomfortable feedback conversations become. With this approach to leadership, feedback conversations are about helping a person to achieve their goals, to grow, and to be the best versions of themselves.

I am very confident you'll find that the meaning and satisfaction you realize from consistently being a coach who is helping team members to thrive far outweighs the short-term pain of taking the time to give regular feedback.

The first step toward meeting the need people have for receiving regular, helpful feedback is to work on building the habit of approaching feedback conversations with the coaching mindset and on having them more frequently. Ideally, a team member shouldn't go more than a week without receiving some type of feedback, whether positive or on areas for growth. In the absence of feedback, team members will assume they're doing well, and poor performance will not likely correct itself.

The feedback should be offered as soon as possible after the event that triggered the feedback. These can be quick, five-minute conversations. Most of your feedback should be reinforcing behaviors you'd like to see more of. If you've been keeping up with your daily reminder to appreciate people for doing things right, you're already halfway there. The appreciation you're sharing definitely counts as feedback.

Whenever necessary, feedback can also be on what could be done better in the future. I recommend having these conversations separately. The approach of the "feedback sandwich"—in which constructive feedback is sandwiched between two pieces of positive feedback—has been shown to be ineffective, and often counterproductive.

Here's a simple way to ensure that team members don't go too long without feedback.

Take a moment right now to update the calendar event you have each day for appreciation, and amend it to be for appreciation and feedback. Then each day when you're reflecting on which team members have done something right, and appreciating them for it, you could also take a minute to think about any team members who haven't received any type of constructive feedback in the last seven days and take some time to provide feedback for them.

If you are already in the habit of providing timely feedback, this new calendar reminder can simply serve as a safeguard to ensure that an important feedback conversation isn't missed.

Feedback That Inspires Greatness

Just as important as providing feedback frequently is providing feedback that is actually helpful. Apparently most managers are regularly failing to do this. Gallup research has also found that only 26 percent of employees say that the feedback they receive is helpful.

The primary reason employees cite for this is that feedback tends to be a one-way conversation, and it feels like criticism or judgment. Great leaders don't criticize or judge because that's not helpful. Research suggests that one-way feedback only improves performance about one-third of the time, and actually makes it worse one-third of the time.

Great leaders coach. They turn feedback conversations into coaching conversations. Coaches ask a lot of questions, and spend less time speaking than the person they are coaching.

Whether we think an assignment went well or not, we should approach the conversation in the spirit of first trying to understand the team member's perspective. This approach is very effective when the issue is the behavior of the team member. And it keeps us open to the possibility that the real issue may actually be a process that needs to be improved, or a lack of necessary resources. Uncovering those types of issues can result in highly leveraged approaches for improving team performance.

I recommend starting the conversation with an open-ended question like, "What are your thoughts about how the assignment went?" If the team member provides a short answer like, "I think it went well," you can simply say, "Great, tell me more about that, please."

If the team member still doesn't provide a lot of detail, you could ask, "What do you think went well?" If they only list one thing, you could ask if there's anything else.

When the team member says there's nothing else, you could then ask, "What do you think could be done better next time?" In many cases, the team member will be able to identify one or more areas that could be improved.

By allowing the team member to share first, at a minimum you're creating a real, two-way conversation, which helps build trust. You're also helping the team member develop self-awareness, which is probably the most important skill there is for both professional and personal success.

And, there's also a chance that you won't need to provide any constructive feedback because the team member will have identified any areas for improvement. Then you can simply follow up by asking what they plan to do differently next time and how you can help set them up for success.

If the team member fails to mention an area that you would like to see improved, here's how I recommend sharing constructive feedback.

1. Adopt a Coaching Mindset

First, the mindset is really important. I recommend approaching feedback with the mindset of wanting to help the team member grow and to excel at what they do because that's what's best for *them*. If you can express this authentically, it can be very helpful to initiate a feedback conversation by saying something like, "I'd like to share some thoughts on helping you hit some of your goals."

Even better, if you can express this authentically, is a preface to feedback that boosts both effort and performance so significantly that the researchers from Stanford, Columbia, and Yale who discovered it call it "wise feedback" that is almost "magical." And it's just one, brief sentence: "I'm giving you these comments because I have very high expectations and I know that you can reach them."

The simple sentence above reinforces that you have the best interests of the team member in mind, and that you truly care about that person.

2. Be Specific and Objective

Second, feedback needs to be specific and objective. Instead of saying things like "You handled that call poorly," which is an opinion that could trigger a feeling of defensiveness, I recommend saying, "On the call, you said _____," which is a specific, objective statement.

Here's another chance to be a coach. You could ask the team member, "What do you think might be a more effective thing to say?"

Again, team members will often realize how to improve when given the chance to reflect. And if they don't think of a way to improve, you can certainly help out there and suggest, "Next time, I'd like you to try this, instead."

3. Connect the Feedback to the Big Picture

Third, to be most helpful, I recommend explaining why the improvement is important and how it will help the team member to see better results and hit a specific team goal or meet a specific expectation. If possible, you could even connect how improving in this area will help the team member to achieve one or more of their personal goals.

4. Be a Resource

Finally, I recommend asking how you could help the team member implement the change. If the team member can't think of a way you could help, you could make a suggestion like doing a practice run with you.

A Better Way to Manage Performance

After you and any managers you lead get some practice with the approach to feedback shared in this chapter, you might want to consider creating a performance management process or system that leverages the power of it. According to research conducted by Gartner, the average manager spends 10 percent of their entire work year on performance management-related tasks. Much of this time is wasted on cumbersome annual review processes that add little or no value in most cases and, in many cases, frustrate both employees and managers and actually reduce the engagement levels of both.

If you set up a performance management system that is aligned with the approach to feedback shared in this chapter, you dramatically reduce the time spent on performance management–related tasks, eliminate one of the most frustrating elements of the workplace, and actually significantly improve both performance and engagement. The performance management process becomes focused on helping people win at work, as Garry Ridge described in his book by the same title, instead of judging them once or twice per year.

If you'd like help setting up a performance management system that follows the approach outlined in this book and utilizes existing technology to further reduce the amount of time employees and managers spend on performance management–related tasks, I'd be happy to help guide you in the process with a free forty-five-minute consultation. To schedule, please visit inspiregreatnessbook.com/performance.

• • • Action Items for Chapter 12 • • •

1. Please update the calendar event you have each day for appreciation, and amend it to be for "appreciation and feedback." Then each day when you're reflecting on which team members have done something right, and appreciating them for it, you could also take a

minute to think about any team members who haven't received any type of feedback in the last seven days and take some time to provide feedback for them, whether it's appreciating what you want to see more of or, if necessary, having a helpful coaching session on an area for growth.

2. Please write out a process for how you'll approach your next feedback conversation, per the guidance in this chapter, and keep it handy to review before that conversation.

13

Giving Power Away

How to Improve Engagement While Simultaneously Freeing Up Tremendous Amounts of Time

Although his father wanted him to be a physician, Antonio Curt Semler was more interested in engineering, and graduated from Vienna's Polytechnic University. Realizing that opportunities were few in Austria at the time, he moved to Argentina in 1937 to work for DuPont.

After a visit to Brazil in 1952, Curt was intrigued by the seemingly endless possibilities of the quickly developing country. He moved to São Paulo and started his own business based on centrifuge technology he had developed that could separate oil from plants.

While his business grew, he married another Austrian immigrant, named Renée. Because he was already in his forties, having children became a priority. After three miscarriages, Renée gave birth to a girl, named Susan, and, eleven months later, a boy, named Ricardo.

Curt's company, called Semco, continued to grow along with the Brazilian economy, which accelerated especially rapidly in the late 1960s and early '70s. This was a period known as the "Brazilian Miracle," when Brazil enjoyed average annual increases in gross domestic product (GDP) of 10 percent. In the '70s, Brazil created a "five-year plan" for creating a shipbuilding industry, and Semco leveraged the opportunity by adding marine pump manufacturing to the business.

With his business, Curt was very interested in creating a legacy, and wanted Semco to be a family business that would last for generations. For multiple reasons, he couldn't imagine his daughter, Susan, leading this type of company. So, when the time came to start preparing his successor, he faced two serious problems.

First, his son, Ricardo, did not seem to be a likely successor to the business. He showed no interest in taking over Semco. And, although he showed potential in both leadership and entrepreneurship, Ricardo was a bit of a rebel who did poorly in school. He preferred spending his time playing the guitar.

Despite his poor grades, Ricardo ended up attending and studying law at São Paulo State Law School, the most prestigious university in Brazil. But it didn't take him long to realize that he was not likely going to be a lawyer. And, not long after, he realized that, despite his passion for the guitar, he probably wasn't going to be a professional guitar player, either. So, he eventually decided to give the family business a try and started working at Semco while still in law school.

His time at Semco did not start off well. Ricardo, a rebel at heart, didn't like the way his father ran the business. Employees weren't happy and there was a lot of bureaucracy. Also, Ricardo didn't think Semco should stay so focused on marine pumps, which had become the core focus of the business.

The second problem Curt Semler faced was that the Brazilian economy—which had boomed in the early 1970s—was entering into a serious recession. If he left Semco, he would be leaving during the most challenging time the company had ever faced.

It was precisely because of the recession that Ricardo wanted to diversify the business. He was worried that since the shipping industry was among the hardest hit in the recession, Semco would be very vulnerable if it wasn't diversified.

Curt and Ricardo argued about almost everything, but the question of diversification was the most important issue. This was so important to Ricardo that he spent a year pursuing the acquisition of a ladder company, even interviewing dozens of potential CEOs, which gave him a world-class education in business.

Knowing that the deal on the ladder company was about to close, and that Ricardo was considering leaving to run the ladder company instead of adding the business to Semco, Curt was concerned that his dream of having the business stay in the family was about to end. Because they argued about everything, Curt knew that he and his son couldn't work together. So, when he asked Ricardo to stay, he offered him the majority of Semco shares, and the authority to make whatever changes he thought he needed to make.

To clarify his understanding, Ricardo asked, "Who's going to run Semco?"

After a long silence, Curt replied, "Better make your mistakes while I'm still alive."

Ricardo wasted no time in mixing things up. He knew that most of the managers at Semco were against diversification, and that if they stayed, the company would likely fail.

Despite being extremely nervous about it, on his first day as a twenty-one-year-old CEO, Ricardo fired fifteen (nearly 60 percent) of the senior leaders at Semco. The next day, he hired one of the people he had interviewed as a potential CEO of the ladder company to help him run Semco.

Within a couple years, Ricardo and the new leadership team had succeeded in saving the company from becoming a victim of the recession in Brazil. Semco was offering new products, had doubled the size of its workforce, and opened a number of new manufacturing plants.

However, Semco was highly focused on numbers. This, along with Ricardo's autocratic leadership style, was taking a toll on the employees. Employees didn't seem motivated. Quality wasn't nearly as good as it could have been. Orders were often shipped late.

Also, Ricardo was running himself into the ground by trying to be in control of everything. He had gained fifty pounds, and suffered from a persistent sore throat and frequent, severe headaches.

But he didn't slow down until he was forced to. While visiting a factory in Baldwinsville, NY, Ricardo collapsed right on the factory floor. He was seen a few days later by a doctor at the Lahey clinic in Boston, MA. After undergoing many tests, Ricardo was sure the doctor would find some type of serious illness.

But the doctor told Ricardo that he found no evidence of any disease. He told Ricardo, "You are suffering from an advanced case of stress. The most advanced case of stress I have ever seen in a person of twenty-five."

The doctor told Ricardo that if he wanted to avoid lots of trips back to see doctors, "absolutely everything about your life has to change."

Ricardo heeded the doctor's advice. He quit working evenings and weekends and started engaging in activities other than work. He eventually instituted what he calls "terminal days." These are weekly workdays that he uses not to work, but to do things he would do if he had received a terminal diagnosis of some type.

Ricardo also changed how he approached leadership and culture. As he explains in his book *Maverick*,

> I had no grand plan. Just a sense that there was a lifelessness, a lack of enthusiasm, a malaise at Semco, and that I had to change it. People weren't gratified by their jobs and often seemed oppressed by them. The traditional attitude about workers was that you couldn't trust them. You needed systems to control them. I wanted to know if it was possible to liberate people and

free them from the elements of life that make it a drag by creating an entirely new kind of organization.

Over the years, with the help of an innovative HR director he hired, the changes he made to his approach to business and leadership were absolutely extraordinary, and all centered around giving up as much control as possible to the employees at Semco. He came to increasingly believe—and found increasing evidence that—the more you empower team members to control as much of their work and their lives as possible, the better the results for the team members *and* the company.

By 1990, employees at Semco set their own dress code (there is none), set their own production quotas, set their own schedules, wrote their own job descriptions, evaluated and hired their managers, and even set their own salaries! The employee handbook was twenty pages long, but consisted mostly of cartoons. The overall message was simply, "We trust you to use common sense."

When employees travel on business trips, there are no rules for spending, and no audits of expense reports. Employees are encouraged to spend what they need to get the job done, as if they were on personal travel using their own money. Ricardo believes that if you can't trust employees to decide what hotel to stay in or which section of a plane to choose, you probably shouldn't trust them to travel to faraway places representing your company.

Ricardo's approach was so radical that even employees sometimes pushed back and asked management to take more control. For instance, after two drills had gone missing at one plant, the employees there asked to have security checks reinstated as people left work for the day.

One union leader said, "Our people want the searches. They want everyone to know that they're not the ones taking the tools." But Ricardo refused to reinstate the security checks, saying, "I would rather have a few thefts once in a while than condemn everyone to a system based on mistrust."

It's difficult to overstate the success that Ricardo has realized with his approach of building a self-governed company with almost no rules. Nine years after Ricardo became CEO, Semco was successfully selling a wide range of products, it was among the top two companies in Brazil in all of its markets, and it was one of the fastest-growing companies in Brazil.

Then, in 1990, the Brazilian economy crashed. It wasn't long before nearly one thousand Brazilian businesses were failing every month. By the end of 1991, sales at Semco had fallen 40 percent from their high in 1989.

Most companies in this situation would resort to layoffs to stay in business. Semco almost did, too, but ultimately took a different approach. Employees came up with a solution to help everyone keep their jobs. They proposed a solution in which they agreed to take a 30 percent pay cut provided that management agreed to take a 40 percent pay cut, profit sharing was increased from 24 to 39 percent, and employees could approve every expenditure to help keep costs down.

In a short time, employees started to see results. The company actually turned a profit after about a month. This inspired the employees to further reduce costs, so they started taking over all the work done by outside contractors, like cleaning bathrooms, driving trucks, and running the cafeteria.

In one of the worst economic times Brazil has ever seen, Semco was not only surviving, but profitable. It wasn't long before all employees started once again receiving their full salaries. And Semco emerged from the recession an even stronger company with a stronger, more loyal workforce that would propel the company to another extraordinary decade of success.

From the time Ricardo Semler took over the company in 1980 to the time he stepped down as CEO and let the employees lead the company without a fixed CEO, the company grew from eighty employees to five thousand employees, grew annual revenues from $4 million to $212 million, and had an annual average growth rate of 47 percent.

Also, Semco has created a workplace that people love and is making a positive impact on their well-being and growth. The average annual turnover rate in the manufacturing industry is often around 40 percent. Semco has consistently had annual turnover rates around 2 percent.

The wife of an employee once came to speak with an HR team member at Semco. She said that her husband had changed. He no longer yelled at the kids, he asked other family members what they wanted to do on weekends, and he was no longer acting like his "usual, grumpy, autocratic self." Ricardo realized that Semco was making a positive impact not only in the lives of employees, but on the community as well.

Perhaps the most telling evidence for the success of Ricardo's approach is that the company continued to grow and thrive after he stepped down as CEO. He had successfully created an organization that was about as autonomous as possible for a for-profit company. It no longer needed him.

Baby Steps Toward More Autonomy

Every leader almost certainly likes the idea of empowering a team or organization to the point where the team or organization functions just as well when the leader is absent as when she is present. However, I have met very few leaders who would be comfortable giving away as much control as Ricardo Semler gave away at Semco.

This is especially true for leaders of publicly traded companies, who are under tremendous pressure to hit profit targets every single quarter. Experimenting with autonomy is likely to be viewed as an extremely risky proposition that could cost a CEO her job.

To be clear, I don't recommend that you, or any other leader of an established organization, necessarily try to replicate what Ricardo Semler has done. I'm confident Ricardo would not recommend that, either.

However, consistently taking small steps toward helping employees on your team to have more autonomy is one of the most powerful habits you can create as a leader. There is an abundance of evidence linking higher levels of autonomy to increased well-being, satisfaction, and engagement. In fact, a solid case can be made that for most modern jobs, autonomy is a better motivator than money.

Having agency or autonomy is a need so important for people that we tend to overlook it. It's just too obvious. We all want to have as much control over our lives as possible.

And this need has been quantified to some degree by scientific research. In self-determination theory, for instance, autonomy is listed as one of the three basic psychological needs for growth and development.

In addition to benefiting employees and the organization as a whole, giving autonomy to employees also benefits managers. The more autonomy that employees have, the less work a manager has to do. Instead of making decisions nonstop all day, every day, they can gradually push most decisions down to employees, freeing up tremendous amounts of time and mental energy.

There are three main areas of work that offer possibilities for giving employees increased levels of autonomy: where they do their work, when they do their work, and how they do their work. Although not all of these areas may apply entirely to your situation, I recommend still exploring the potential of each, as it may help spark some ideas for another area.

Autonomy Regarding How Work Is Done

Although people tend not to mind being assigned tasks, almost no one enjoys being told how to do those tasks. Managers are well served by refraining, as much as possible, from telling employees how to do their work. And, in the long term, the goal could be to allow employees, as much as possible, to even decide what they work on.

I recommend starting this journey with a simple habit for giving employees more autonomy regarding how they do their work. Whenever team members come to you to ask for help or for permission with something, I recommend making it a habit to ask them to tell you what they think they should do, and to explain the thinking behind their approach. You can certainly guide the direction of the conversation with your questions, but try to ask as many open-ended questions as needed to allow team members to come up with a solution on their own. After an employee has come up with an effective solution to a certain type of issue two more times, it may be an opportune moment to let him know that he no longer needs to ask you for permission for that particular issue.

Just as with the approach to responding to ideas you learned in chapter eleven, this takes some additional time at first. But, if you continue this habit with every employee for a while, there could come a time when employees no longer need to ask you for permission for anything, and no longer ask for your help with anything. Imagine how much time this could free up for you!

Perhaps more important, this habit will lay the foundation for gradually giving employees more and more autonomy over many more aspects of their work lives, potentially even what they work on and where and when they do their work. The more that employees have a say about where they work, when they work, what the office looks like, how they do their work, and so on, the more they will feel and act like owners of the company, making decisions on their own, with the best interests of the company in mind.

This is why providing employees with autonomy is among the most highly leveraged activities leaders can engage in. Providing autonomy saves tremendous amounts of time, dramatically improves engagement and productivity, and simultaneously meets one of the most important basic needs people have for thriving.

Autonomy Regarding Where Work Is Done

Many organizations have brick-and-mortar locations where customers are served, or products are made. Of course, in those cases, it's not possible to immediately allow employees to work where they choose. However, this is certainly something that could be offered to employees who are promoted from frontline positions. Also, if and when there comes a time when a new office, store, or plant opens up, affected employees could be involved in the process of choosing the location.

For those employees who do not need to be in a specific place to do their jobs, there is much debate about the ideal policy for working location. Should team members be allowed to work 100 percent virtually? Should they be required to work in the office? Should there be a hybrid policy that outlines how many days employees should be in the office and how many they should be virtual?

This debate is predicated on a flawed assumption: that employees don't have the ability to figure this out for themselves. Thus, any "policy" we create regarding working location is going to keep us from maximizing employee well-being and engagement because it's unnecessarily stripping employees of autonomy over a very important area of their lives. Employees don't want a policy to dictate where and when they work. They want to be seen as adults who can be trusted to figure this out for themselves.

Autonomy Regarding When Work Is Done

Much like physical location, when people work may be best for them to decide. As long as clear performance goals are established (ideally with employee involvement), why shouldn't employees be allowed to decide when they do the work required to achieve those goals?

If employees are gradually empowered to make more decisions for themselves, and to think like owners of a business, this type of autonomy can even be offered to manufacturing and service jobs. For instance, at Semco, workers in manufacturing plants were allowed to come in at any time between 7 AM and 9 AM. At first, this probably sounds crazy to most readers. One would likely wonder what would happen if one teammate decided to start at seven and another at nine. Wouldn't that be a major disruption?

The leaders at Semco were concerned about that, too, so they set up a task force to help mediate any problems that came up. The task force never needed to meet. The employees knew that they wouldn't hit production goals (goals they set for themselves) if they didn't coordinate their schedules with each other, so they coordinated their schedules with each other.

The employees at the plant were treated like adults who can be trusted to figure out things like schedules on their own, and they did.

• • • Action Items for Chapter 13 • • •

1. Create a daily, five-minute calendar event to remind you to practice asking people what they intend to do and why anytime an employee asks you for help with something or asks your permission to do something.
2. Write a plan for how you could give team members more autonomy over how, where, and when they do their work.
3. Reach out to a few of your peers and schedule a time to chat about your ideas and, if necessary, create a plan for how managers could request more autonomy over decisions like where and when people work.

14

Helping People Grow

A Simple Way to Unlock Potential

Cindy Wang is a very talented engineer with an impressive resume. After working as an individual contributor for fifteen years at some of the most innovative companies in the US, she wanted to grow to become a leader, so she took on a management role. When she joined her current company, a tech giant with nearly twenty thousand employees, her first role was leading a team of senior systems and network engineers.

Although still relatively new as a manager, Cindy was able to help her team achieve excellent results. A number of times, Cindy's team was able to successfully accomplish objectives that other teams had failed to accomplish. She was consistently rated as a top performer.

Despite the results that Cindy and her team achieved, Cindy was repeatedly passed up for promotions. She was told that it would "just be a matter of time," that she was "doing a great job," and she should keep doing what she was doing.

But Cindy really wanted to grow into a senior manager role, and she knew that there must be reasons for why she wasn't getting promoted. If someone would just tell her what those reasons were, she was ready and willing to do the work to overcome the deficiencies.

Cindy was growing increasingly frustrated, so she moved to another team in the company, hoping that she would be able to grow and be promoted there. But the experience was like déjà vu. Cindy and her team achieved excellent results, but she was passed over for promotions again.

Feeling even more frustrated, she asked her direct manager what she needed to improve in order to become a senior manager. Cindy's manager replied, "Let me put some thought into that and get back to you." The manager never got back to Cindy with an answer.

Cindy was so hungry for growth, but it seemed that no one wanted to invest in her. She eventually became so frustrated that she started to seriously consider leaving the company. In fact, after a particularly frustrating experience with her supervisor, she reached out to a director of another team, named Aaron Nichols, telling him she was planning to leave, and asking for his advice.

Aaron is well aware of Cindy's talents and saw potential in her as a leader. He knows she is a valuable asset to the company. He asked her if she would stay with the company if he could bring her to his team and invest in her growth.

Cindy has a lot of respect for Aaron and believed that he was genuinely interested in helping her grow. Cindy decided to stay and, not long after, was able to join Aaron's team.

Aaron believed that the best way to help Cindy to grow her abilities to lead other managers was to put her in a senior manager role with managers reporting to her. This would allow him to get valuable feedback from Cindy's direct reports on where she is strong, and where she has room to grow.

Thus, Aaron made Cindy a senior manager on his team and got to work helping her grow. Almost immediately, Cindy's direct reports were providing feedback to her that she was micromanaging them. However, unaccustomed to receiving constructive feedback, she didn't respond to the feedback well. She continued to micromanage.

Not long after, Aaron gave Cindy similar feedback and let her know that if she wanted to grow, she would need to do some work on several essential leadership skills. He said, "If you're willing to do the work, I'm more than willing to invest in you, Cindy."

Although it's almost never easy to receive constructive feedback, and she would need some practice to apply feedback to growing, Cindy was internally rejoicing. *Finally*, she thought, *someone is willing to let me know what I need to do to grow.*

Over the next couple of years, Cindy worked harder than ever, particularly on growth. She worked with a coach. She worked with several mentors. And she became much more open to feedback from her team members.

In fact, she seemed to develop a craving for constructive feedback. She started asking for feedback on almost every area of her work. Nowadays, she seems to almost always be asking, "How did I do? What could I be doing better?"

Three years after joining Aaron Nichols's team, Cindy Wang was promoted to be a director and, as of this writing, is successfully leading a team of thirty people.

I asked Cindy how working with a leader who invests in her growth has affected her. She replied, "I have grown so much over the last few years that I feel like I am a completely different person now. This growth has been so fulfilling and energizing."

"Energizing?" I asked.

"Yes," she said. "I used to work hard because I felt I had to get noticed and to have a chance of getting promoted. Now, I work even harder and constantly seek out new challenges and ways to add value for my team and the company, not because I feel like I have to, but because I genuinely want to."

If We're Not Growing, We're Dying

For some time now, the Gallup organization has conducted some very interesting research on what people feel is necessary for them to live "the best life imaginable." Historically, people have tended to prioritize some very important aspects of life, like safety, followed by adequate food and shelter, then starting a family, owning a home, and living in peace.

In the last few years, another important aspect of life has jumped up in the rankings, and it may surprise you. For the average person, having a great job is now viewed as more important than owning a home, getting married, and starting a family! Fortunately, Gallup has also done extensive research into what makes a job "great."

The research from Gallup has shown that two general core needs are the most important drivers of people feeling like they have a great job. One of these needs is growth. (You'll learn about the other need in chapter eighteen.)

The universal need to be continuously growing as a person is so powerful that it may have an impact not just on our psychological well-being, but on our physical well-being, too. It's been said that if "we're not growing, we're dying." Although this phrase tends to be thought of as an analogy, there's some evidence that this may literally be true.

A now famous study on the effects of aging on the brain, which began in 1986 at the University of Minnesota by David Snowdon, tracked many details of the lives of 678 elderly Catholic nuns living in School Sisters of Notre Dame convents across the United States. The researchers recorded many details of the nuns' daily lives for years. And, after the sisters passed away, the researchers examined the sisters' brains.

The first set of results published from this research received a tremendous amount of attention from other researchers and the media. It turns out that nearly one-third of the brains of the deceased sisters showed signs of Alzheimer's disease, such as increased amounts of amyloid plaques and tau tangles.

But the study didn't garner attention because one-third of participants clearly had the biological hallmarks of Alzheimer's. It received attention because those sisters weren't dying of Alzheimer's, and they hadn't shown any signs of Alzheimer's while they were alive.

As part of the study, the sisters received regular cognitive evaluations. These evaluations are so effective that neurologists can often diagnose Alzheimer's before they see any brain imaging that could confirm their diagnosis.

Yet these nuns, whose brains had clear pathological evidence of Alzheimer's when they were studied after death, had all passed their cognitive evaluations with flying colors. One of these nuns, who was examined several times while in her eighties before dying of a heart attack at age eighty-five, could tell the current time—without looking at her watch—with a margin of error of roughly four minutes, while many of her "healthy" peers couldn't accurately determine whether it was morning or afternoon.

How could this be? How could these nuns survive, and even thrive, despite having brains riddled with one of the most ruthless diseases in the world?

The answers were discovered after looking at the activity levels of the nuns. Researchers noticed that the nuns who had the pathology of Alzheimer's, but showed no symptoms of the disease while they were alive, had remained engaged in constant growth by maintaining important responsibilities, learning new skills, and teaching others. By continuing to grow, it appears, the nuns protected their brains from the devastating effects of Alzheimer's.

The Power of Helping Team Members Grow

When Cindy Wang was on a team with a leader who didn't help her grow, she felt stifled and frustrated. Although she worked hard, because that's just who she is, it is unlikely that she lived up to her potential or was as effective at creative problem-solving as she could be. By simply moving to a team with a leader that helped her grow, she flourished.

There were likely several factors that contributed to Cindy thriving on the team led by Aaron Nichols. The two most important were:

1. that Aaron invested in Cindy's growth, which
2. demonstrated that he cared about her.

Feeling cared for by one's manager is no doubt the most powerful driver of employee engagement. But, as Cindy told me when I spoke with her, the experience of growing itself is very energizing. People are energized, and more likely to be fully engaged, when they are growing.

This may help explain why people can become obsessed with relatively useless hobbies like playing tennis, or golf, or chess. Almost no one who regularly plays tennis, or golf, or chess is ever going to be a champion, and most get frustrated often at how poorly they play. But there's something energizing about the pursuit of getting better—just for the sake of growing—that energizes people to work to get better at these games.

In addition to anecdotal evidence, there is also a large body of research that quantifies the benefits of helping team members to grow. According to Gallup, only one out of every three employees strongly agrees that they have opportunities at work to learn and grow. And, by doubling that ratio, organizations could realize *14 percent higher productivity.*

Although 14 percent higher productivity may sound like an exaggeration, there is a clear connection between growing team members and growing an organization. By helping team members grow, leaders are not only helping people to be more engaged (arguably the best predictor of growth); they are also helping increase the capacity of the organization.

There are only a few ways to grow the capacity of an organization. We can improve the strategy. We can improve tactics and processes for executing the strategy. We can improve the engagement levels of the people executing the strategy. And we can increase the effectiveness of the people executing the strategy. For instance, one really good software engineer is often as productive as five to ten average software engineers.

I can only think of two ways to increase the effectiveness of the people executing a strategy. We can hire new people, or we can grow the people who are currently on the team. In the short term, hiring new people may be necessary sometimes. Over the long term, however, growing the people we have is the more efficient and more enjoyable approach.

Strategic Delegation

In chapter thirteen, you already learned two habits for growing team members: regularly coaching them to solve problems on their own and gradually reducing the number of activities that require team members to ask for permission. These habits serve team members well by helping them to develop decision-making skills and autonomy, and they help the leader save a lot of time in the long term.

A habit that creates a similar win-win situation is strategic delegation. Many leaders know that to be most effective they need to delegate as much work as possible to team members so the leader can focus on strategic thinking and inspiring greatness in team members. By being strategic with delegation, leaders can simultaneously help team members to grow, while also helping *themselves* to grow.

Before diving into the details of the strategy, it's important to understand the mindset behind growing team members through delegation. The goal, which sounds counterintuitive, is to make yourself replaceable, as Aaron Anderson, whom you met in chapter five, became addicted to doing.

For most managers—who are almost always promoted because they are "A players" who are really good at their jobs—this can sound quite scary. But if you can create a situation where you could take two weeks off without notice, and your team could still keep its promises to internal and external customers, that is actually a sign of great leadership.

When you grow a team like this, it frees you up to spend even more time on strategy, process improvement, and making more consistently positive impacts on the well-being and growth of your team members. And this is a strong indication that you are actually ready for more senior leadership responsibilities or positions, when those opportunities arise.

To be more strategic with delegation, I recommend an approach I learned from my colleague Mike Figliuolo when I interviewed him. The first step is to make a list of all the things you currently do that are required for your job and things you'd like to do as part of your own growth. You can break these into four categories:

1. Tasks that are very easy for you
2. Tasks that you're comfortable with but take some work and thought
3. Tasks you can do but require a good deal of work and thought
4. New tasks that you'd like to take on, that you don't know how to do now

All the tasks that fall into the first category should be delegated or, if they're not adding value, eliminated. When deciding which tasks to delegate to which team members, try to match tasks to areas you know team members would like to grow in. Although that might not be possible for all the tasks, it's worth doing the best you can. You can learn about where team members would like to grow in one-to-one conversations you have, or you could have them complete this assignment, too.

You may not be able to delegate all the tasks in the second category: tasks that you're comfortable with but take some work and thought. For those that you can delegate, again, try to match them to areas in which team members are looking to grow.

Another element to consider when delegating is the bandwidth of your team members. If you're delegating tasks to them that are in the fourth category for them—new tasks that they'd like to take on, that they don't know how to do now—you need to ensure that they're not overloaded. You may need to help them delegate some of their current tasks from the first category to more junior team members.

Also, before you delegate a task that falls in the second category for you, you need to make sure you have the bandwidth to coach team members and, to whatever degree is necessary, help them succeed with the tasks you delegate. It's important to ask them to create a plan for how they'll complete the project so they fully understand the goal and are more likely to retain what they learn. Remember, this is a short-term investment that can free up a lot of your time in the long run.

Tasks and activities that fall in the third category for you should probably not be delegated unless the task or activity is in an area in which you are weak and a team member is strong. If you can have the humility to allow a direct report to be better than you at something, delegating these types of tasks and activities can free up a lot of mental energy and make your work more fulfilling by allowing you to focus on your strengths. Also, this can help prepare you for higher levels of management, in which most of the people on your team will have greater domain expertise than you.

Once you've delegated as many of the tasks and activities from the first three categories as possible, you'll have more time to take on new responsibilities in the fourth category, in addition to having more time to think strategically and help team members to thrive.

Mastering One's Role

Another way for leaders to help team members to grow is to give them the learning time they need to become masters of their current role, which is one of the best investments leaders can make. The learning time I'm referring to here is ongoing learning that happens after team members have finished their initial training. In addition to being very valuable for your team members, this is another highly leveraged way to add value for your team or organization by expanding its capacity.

I recommend creating a structured plan for allowing team members to put at least one hour per week on the calendar to take a break from executing tasks and focus entirely on learning. During this time, they should also not be expected to respond to any non-urgent communication like email or chat. Ideally, I recommend allowing team members to choose their own topics for learning, as long as it's somehow related to helping them grow in their role, which is yet another way to offer autonomy.

To help reinforce the learning, I recommend asking team members to send you an email each week with a paragraph or so explaining what they learned and how they might apply it. If you like, at least some of the time, you could take this a step further and have team members teach what they learned to you and their teammates with a quick ten- to fifteen-minute class. This helps team members develop communication skills and helps develop the rest of the team all at once.

Be an Investor in People

As a business owner, I used to get frustrated when I felt that newer team members weren't being as productive as I wanted them to be. My mind would have ideas constantly flashing through it like, *I can't believe I'm paying this person $70,000 per year. They're not producing anywhere near that amount of value.*

I eventually grew to see things differently. I've realized that hiring people is a long-term investment. And I now see investing in human beings as the best investment there is.

By providing people with a livelihood, and investing in helping them to grow, I've realized that the likelihood of not getting a good financial return from the investment is very low. However, even if the investment in one particular person were to break even, or produce a financial loss, the return of happiness is *guaranteed*. It is incredibly fulfilling to help people grow.

As a point of comparison, consider investing in the stock market. The best investors are happy to realize a 15–20 percent average annual return before accounting for inflation, and there's almost zero chance they're going to realize the fulfillment of seeing a human being grow and thrive as a result of their investment. However, engaged employees often produce annual returns of 500 to 1,000 percent or more. And these financial returns are accompanied by the joy and fulfillment of serving and inspiring greatness in team members. As a result of these realizations, I prefer to invest in people whenever possible.

One effective and fulfilling way to invest in people is to provide them with regular training, above and beyond what they receive during onboarding, or the hour per week they engage in during self-directed training. Investing in training team members is one way to simultaneously meet the human need for growth while also meeting the need to feel that one's manager cares about them. This is especially true when the training helps the team members in their personal lives. Here's how I recommend achieving this.

At least once every six months, managers should offer at least one in-depth training on a topic that will help team members grow professionally, or one that will help them grow personally. In many cases, professional and personal development can overlap. For instance, training on topics such as organizational skills, time management, communication, listening, and self-awareness and other emotional intelligence competencies can help team members be much more effective at work and in their personal lives.

However, there is something special about offering training from time to time that is mostly or entirely focused on personal growth and development. This can go a long way to helping team members know that we truly care about them as people. And, of course, even training that is 100 percent focused on personal growth actually still benefits the team or organization.

Remember, team members are human beings, and we get the whole human being at work. A happier, healthier team member is going to be significantly more engaged and productive than a team member who is miserable and unhealthy.

The training you offer doesn't have to require any financial invest-ment. It could be you teaching a class. It could be reading a book a quar-ter as a team, on company time, and having a few group discussions on it. Ideally, at least some of the training should be either based on what the team has expressed an interest in, or customized for each individual based on their professional and personal goals, and could include online courses, books, or even being connected with mentors internal or exter-nal to the organization.

By investing time, and even money, in helping team members to grow, you're not only making a sound investment in the success of your team or organization. You're helping people live "their best life imag-inable" by helping them have a "great" job. Can you think of a better investment than that?

• • • Action Items for Chapter 14 • • •

1. Set a thirty-minute calendar event for once each quarter to complete the exercise on strategic delegation, as described in this chapter.

2. Write out a brief plan for how you'll help team members put at least one hour per week on their calendars for learning. Add to the plan your thoughts for how you'll ask team members to let you know what they learned, and how you'll determine how often and which topics might be good opportunities to have a team member teach a class on what they learned.

3. Write out a brief plan for how you'd like to offer regular training for team members.

4. Create a twenty-minute event on your calendar for some time in the next week or so to plan out at least one training program in the next six months, even if it's as simple as a book that you all read.

5. Create a twenty-minute event on your calendar for sometime this quarter, which repeats once per quarter, to remind you to plan out some type of training.

15

Building Trust

The Essential Foundation for High Performance

The last job I had before becoming a full-time social entrepreneur in 2011 was with a company called Infinite Energy, headquartered in Gainesville, Florida. I had heard such great things about this company, which had about five hundred employees at the time, that I took an entry-level inside sales position when I started there in 2008, just to get my foot in the door.

About two months after I started working there, I was invited to a lunch for all the people hired in the last ninety days. The lunch was hosted by the founders of the company, Darin Cook and Rich Blaser. During the meeting, Darin and Rich spent a lot of time talking about how they built the company on the basic principle that doing the right thing is always more important than money, and they discussed their values in great detail.

During the year that followed, the message of doing the right thing no matter what the financial cost was reinforced many times. For example, as part of the introduction to a sales training I attended, Darin and

Rich told the story of how they once had to fire the best salesperson in the company because he wasn't acting with high levels of integrity.

Not long after that training, I remember a "letter from the CEO" that Darin sent out to the company that reinforced the values and also challenged all employees to do what is ethical, no matter how much doing the right thing would cost the company. The example that stood out the most to me, though, was an inspiring decision they had made just a few years before I joined the company.

For consumers who are in deregulated markets, one of the advantages of buying their energy from a company like Infinite Energy, instead of directly from the utility company (which only offers a variable rate), is that most energy companies are willing to offer fixed rates for periods like one year, three years, or five years. This allows consumers, especially commercial consumers that use a lot of natural gas or electricity, to lock in a good price when prices are low. This can help consumers save a lot of money and be able to forecast their energy expense with an exact number for a long period of time, which helps them reduce variable risk.

One of the states in which Infinite Energy sold energy was New Jersey. When the company first entered the New Jersey market, the only product it sold was a one-year fixed rate. For the aforementioned reasons, this product was very popular, especially as winter was approaching and consumers knew that prices with the utility company were likely to go up.

One year in the fall, not long after Infinite Energy entered the New Jersey market, the utilities in New Jersey decided that they were going to lock the price of energy through the winter. They weren't offering a new product; they had just made an internal decision to lock rates. So, the rate lock wasn't announced to the public.

However, energy suppliers like Infinite Energy were informed about the rate lock. Darin and Rich were faced with what could be a difficult decision for leaders. They felt that they would either have to pull their only product in New Jersey, the one-year fixed rate, or they would be selling to consumers on a false pretense.

The way to sell a fixed rate is to point out that, by purchasing energy from the utility, prices could rise significantly in the winter, as they usually do, and the benefit of going with Infinite Energy's one-year fixed rate is that it allows the consumer to eliminate the risk of prices going up and to better plan cash flows. But Darin and Rich, the marketing team, and the salespeople would all know that there was zero risk prices could go up if the consumer purchased energy from the utility because the utilities had locked their prices through the winter.

What would make this a difficult decision for some leaders is the little detail about the utilities not publicly announcing that they would be locking the rates through the winter. Consumers would probably never know about this.

For Darin and Rich, the decision was not difficult. It was easy. They knew that selling their one-year fixed rate on a false premise—even if the consumer would never know about it—was something that was not aligned with their values. They decided, without much deliberation, to pull their one-year fixed rate from the New Jersey market.

In the short term, their decision probably cost the company tens of millions of dollars in lost revenue, and significant reduction in the speed with which they would gain market share. In the long term, their decision created extraordinary, positive impacts on the company culture, which probably helped unlock enormous amounts of capacity that a weaker culture would never be capable of. By consistently reinforcing their values around doing the right thing, and consistently living those values, Darin and Rich created a culture in which employees had very high levels of trust in them, and in their team members.

Trust Is Rocket Fuel

Trusting the people around us is one of the most fundamental universal needs for being able to thrive, especially at work. When there is a lack of trust in leaders, or one's team members, it's just a matter of time before the team or organization will fail. When people don't trust each other, they spend way too much of their precious mental and physical energy engaged in protecting themselves from the potential threats, not just outside their teams, but within them.

Conversely, when people trust their leaders and team members, all the energy that is tied up in self-preservation in weaker cultures is applied toward accomplishing the mission. It's difficult to overstate just how important this is because it creates such a powerful synergistic effect.

When trust is absent, individuals not only apply less overall energy to accomplishing the team's mission, they also focus more on their own individual efforts. This makes them less likely to see the bigger picture and work well as a team.

But when there is trust, individuals apply much more overall energy, and much more of that energy is directed toward working together as a team. And, at the risk of stating the obvious, a team of people working together well will produce results extraordinarily greater than any individual, and much greater than the sum of the individual efforts.

According to a report published in Great Place To Work, firms with a high-trust environment—where employees can collaboratively and transparently share knowledge—realize stock returns two to three times higher than the industry average and have 50 percent lower turnover rates than competitors.

Building high levels of trust on your team starts with the leaders. And there are three essential elements for leaders to consider. They must provide consistent examples of integrity, they need to be as transparent as possible, and they need to extend trust to others. When leaders consistently do all three of these things, team members trust leaders and are much more likely to behave in ways that build trust among their peers.

Be a Living Example of Integrity

Although there are many definitions of integrity, I believe that integrity has three core components, which are as follows:

1. I Do What I Say I'm Going to Do

A very simple and easy way to build trust is to do what you say you're going to do. And there are two simple habits for consistently doing this.

First, be on time. Every time someone shows up late for something, a little bit of trust is lost in that person. A common thought, which you've likely had, is, *If I can't trust them to be where they say they're going to be, can I trust them with other things?*

I recommend building the habit of being where you say you're going to be early. In addition to ensuring that you're on time even if an unexpected event causes a little delay, when you actually arrive early you can relax and be in a better state of mind to interact with people. Instead of trying to fill the last few minutes with one more email or text message, I recommend just simply sitting or walking in mindfulness, aware of your mind and body while you sit or walk.

Second, don't say yes to anything unless you are 100 percent sure that, absent some extremely unlikely, unforeseen event, you'll actually be able to do what you say yes to. People who like to please others often say yes to things without considering how realistic it is to follow through.

I recommend building the habit of asking follow-up questions when someone asks you to do something. This buys some time for you to think about how realistic it is for you to follow through, and provides additional details to help you with your decision. Those details also open up the possibility of giving a partial "yes." You may not be able to personally do all of what the person is asking of you, but you may be able to help in some way without overcommitting yourself.

2. I Tell the Truth, Even When It's Painful to Do So

For the most part, this is pretty simple. What we say is either true or not true. However, I recommend going a step further and building the habit of being as precise as possible with language by stating that you're uncertain about something if you're not 100 percent certain about it.

This is something my sister has helped me with a lot. I used to state things I had heard as facts without thoroughly researching them, and she did a great job of consistently calling me out when I did.

For example, a volunteer at a park in Gainesville, Florida, in which alligators freely roam all over, told me that if an alligator were to chase me, I should run in a zigzag, because alligators are very fast but can't turn sharply. Trusting the source, I began repeating this as fact. But it's false.

First, the premise is mostly false. From my understanding after further research, it's extremely unlikely that an alligator would chase a person on land in daylight (unless they had been fed by a human). Alligators don't hunt like that. Apparently, they hunt mostly at dusk or nighttime by waiting in the water for an animal to approach the shore, and then thrashing their tails to quickly lunge at the prey, grab it, and pull it into the water to drown it.

Second, even if an alligator did try to chase a person on land, it seems that the best course of action would be to run as fast as you can in a straight line to avoid being caught by the alligator. Apparently, although alligators can accelerate extremely rapidly in the water using their strong tails, their top speed running on land is only ten to eleven miles per hour.

If we make a habit of stating things as facts that are not actually facts—like running in a zigzag is the best way to get away from an alligator that's chasing you—people trust us less. Conversely, by simply offering caveats when we're not sure, like, "I think _____," or, "Although I'm not sure, there seems to be good evidence for _____," or, "I read something about _____ that seemed to make sense and be credible, but I haven't researched it further, so I'm not sure it's correct," we consistently build trust with others.

When people I know who usually offer caveats for their statements don't offer a caveat, I'm very confident that what they're saying is a fact. They've earned my trust with their habit of only stating they're sure about something when they actually are.

3. I Don't Compromise My Values, or the Values of My Team or Organization, for Personal or Financial Gain

One of the quickest ways to erode trust is to say that we value something, and do something opposite of that value. Conversely, a simple way for leaders to build trust is to consistently live the values of the organization, and their own. This builds the trust that people have in leaders, it inspires team members to do the same, and it can unlock a lot of energy from inspiration that leads to high levels of engagement.

Think of how you feel when someone acts with very high levels of character by doing the right thing when it's hard to do so. Don't you feel inspired and energized, and more loyal to that person?

I distinctly remember feeling all these things when I heard about how Darin and Rich decided to pull their one-year-fixed-rate product from the New Jersey market. This example of the Infinite Energy founders so courageously living their values built up an incredible amount of trust in Darin and Rich, and the employees around me. This was a team I was proud to be a part of and that inspired me to consistently do and be my best.

In fact, the only reason I left Infinite Energy was because a nonprofit I had founded grew to the point where I was needed full-time there. If that hadn't happened, I would probably still be working with the team Darin and Rich built.

The Power of Transparency

When talented employees are asked in surveys what they look for in a workplace culture, transparency is often one of the most important elements. However, many managers are reluctant to be transparent because they worry that they'll look less authoritative or more vulnerable.

As a result, according to research conducted by the American Psychological Association, only about half of workers believe that their employer is open and up front with them, and nearly one in four employees don't trust their employer. Clearly, there's a big opportunity to attract top talent simply by being more transparent, along with many other benefits.

First, the more information team members have, the better equipped they are to solve important problems. In fact, one could argue that one of the most important tools team members need to do their jobs is access to information.

When leaders withhold information from team members, they can significantly inhibit engagement and performance. When team members have access to as much information as the C-suite, they tend to feel and think more like owners of the organization.

Imagine a scenario in which a company is struggling and may have to consider layoffs. If a leader withholds that information, they limit the number of people working to solve the problem, and may very well be forced to lay people off. However, if the leader immediately tells the team members about the situation and asks for their help, the chances of solving the problem go up dramatically.

As you may recall from chapter thirteen, this is exactly what happened when the leaders at Semco were so transparent with their team members during an economic downturn. They were consistently transparent with their financial situation, they had helped employees develop a solid level of literacy regarding financial statements, and they had helped employees develop their strategic decision-making skills. The result was that those employees came up with a solution that avoided layoffs and helped Semco turn a profit within thirty days while most Brazilian companies struggled to stay alive and thousands went out of business.

Being transparent about struggles could even result in a lasting improvement that actually grows the organization. Something very similar happened with Southwest Airlines years ago.

When the leadership team found out they were likely to have an unprofitable quarter, they told everyone in the company and asked them to save five dollars per day for the rest of the quarter. Team members ended up saving twice as much as a result of some innovative solutions uncovered by frontline people like baggage handlers. Some of those innovations helped Southwest routinely turn their airplanes around roughly twice as fast as other airlines at the time, saving the company roughly $2.5 billion per year.

Being transparent also helps managers appear more human to team members and strengthens the bonds between managers and employees, which is a key driver of employee engagement. And, when managers set the example by being transparent and vulnerable, team members tend to follow suit.

This means teams have much healthier dynamics that foster psychological safety and well-being. It also means that managers are far more likely to hear about problems quickly, when they're much easier to solve, before they become big problems.

I recommend sharing any information that the C-suite and other managers have access to, with the exception of team members' salaries and information with low degrees of certainty. (As a side note, some companies have experimented with sharing salary information, with mixed results. Semco is one example where this seems to have been effective.)

I also recommend sharing time-sensitive information, whether it's good or bad, as soon as possible, ideally during a team meeting that allows for some back-and-forth and greater nuance. For information that isn't time sensitive, I recommend creating a place where employees can easily find it whenever they'd like to.

Building Trust by Extending Trust

The third essential component of building trust is to extend trust to others, by both being transparent with information and trusting team members to make important decisions with that information.

For example, the CEO of a manufacturing company, along with his executive team, had worked very hard to create a new compensation plan for the sales team. They spent hours and hours trying to get every detail just right and create a compensation plan that people would love.

During a large sales meeting, the CEO proudly announced the new plan with excitement and optimism. However, as he was about halfway through announcing the new plan, he was noticing a lot of grumbling in the audience. He asked, "You don't like the new comp plan?"

The resounding reply was an emphatic, "No!"

Although he was disappointed that all the hard work the executive team put into creating the plan was wasted, he saw an opportunity for a learning moment. After thinking a bit, the CEO said, "Okay. Let's do this. We'll break for three hours. During that time, you'll create a comp plan that you're happy with."

The salespeople looked around, a bit surprised.

The CEO continued, "Before you start, I want you to know that whatever plan you come up with as a team is preapproved. I trust you to create a great plan that's a win-win. Just remember that everyone else's pay in the company will be affected by your plan."

Two hours later, the sales team was ready with a plan they thought was very fair, and that would incentivize high levels of performance. The plan they had created would actually cost the company less than the plan the executive team had created.

When we extend trust to people, two powerful things happen.

First, they tend to live up to the expectation. In other words, when people feel trusted, they tend to act more trustworthy. The more often people act in trustworthy ways, the more likely it will be that acting in trustworthy ways becomes their default behavior. Thus, frequently extending trust can help build a team full of people who trust each other.

As you may recall from chapter thirteen, Ricardo Semler extended trust to Semco employees to make all types of important decisions, and the company thrived. People lived up to the expectations Ricardo had of them despite knowing that they didn't have to. Ricardo had made it clear that employees would continue making decisions regardless of the outcomes. The employees consistently did the right thing and made great decisions not because they *had to*, but because they *wanted to*.

Second, extending trust is a great way to build the trust others have in you. Who would you trust more, someone who doesn't seem to trust anyone around them, or someone who consistently demonstrates trust in others?

An easy way to extend trust more often is to build the habit you learned in chapter thirteen, gradually giving up decision-making authority to employees.

• • • **Action Items for Chapter 15** • • •

1. Please take a moment to write out your own definition of integrity, and include measurable behaviors that are binary (they either happen or they don't).

2. Create a ten-minute calendar event with a notification that pops up on your phone and repeats every evening for the next thirty days. During this time, please reflect on any personal or company core values, including integrity, that you didn't live up to during the day. Then, commit to living them better tomorrow. Finally, think of the times you did live the values and notice how it feels to be aware of that.

3. Think of any information you've withheld from team members recently and why. Then, write out a plan for how and what information you'll share with them and keep it someplace easy to find.

16

Truly Caring

The Most Powerful Driver of Engagement

In January of 2016, Meghann Dawson made a big career change that was both exciting and a little bittersweet. She had spent over a decade at the Credit Union National Association (CUNA) working in roles related to learning and events. She particularly loved planning events and finding keynote speakers for the conferences she helped plan.

Meghann and I actually first met after she hired me to be the keynote speaker at a large CUNA event, and we've been friends ever since. She is extremely smart and talented. She's also incredibly caring and kind. Meghann is one of the finest human beings I have ever met.

Although she knew that she would deeply miss working in the learning space, Meghann was offered a role at CUNA Mutual Group, which is part of the CUNA family of businesses. She saw a lot of potential for new learning and growth there, and accepted the position.

She eagerly jumped into her new role with the positive energy she is known for exuding essentially all the time. And, about two years after joining CUNA Mutual, Meghann was offered a position on a brand-new team responsible for developing a new area of the business from the ground up. It was like being part of a startup.

Meghann was tasked with taking the lead on developing the operating model for the team. She loved the intellectual stimulation of her new role. She also loved working with her new manager, Andrea Naef. Andrea seemed to make the well-being of team members the top priority, and quickly developed meaningful relationships with team members, including Meghann.

But the transition into her new role turned out to be another bittersweet experience. Around the same time she started her new adventure, Meghann learned that her grandfather, who was the principal father figure in her life, had been diagnosed with late-stage, terminal lung cancer. And because "Dadad," as she affectionately called him, lived in New Jersey, and Meghann lived in Wisconsin, she often felt a calling to go spend more time with him.

On one Thursday night, about three months into her new role, Meghann was driving home from a trip to the movie theater to work extra hours on an important presentation of the new model. She and her team had been working on this presentation for months, and the deadline was upon them. It was scheduled to be delivered to the senior leadership team the following Monday.

On her way home, Meghann received a phone call from her mom, who was calling to let Meghann know that Dadad's health was getting worse faster than previously expected. Doctors said he still might have months to live, but his time was running out.

Meghann shared the news with Andrea the next morning. Because she didn't want to let her team down, she told Andrea that she planned to leave for New Jersey on Tuesday morning, after the presentation to the senior leadership team.

Andrea's first thought was to postpone the meeting to give Meghann time to go see her grandfather, but she wasn't sure how the VP who led the senior leadership team would respond. She hadn't interacted with this VP much. It's possible that postponing could have had serious consequences. However, she also didn't want to have the meeting without

Meghann there because she wanted to be sure Meghann received the credit for all of her hard work.

In a matter of seconds, because Andrea believed that allowing Meghann to spend precious time with her Dadad was even more important than the presentation, she made her decision. She told Meghann, "You need to go be with him as soon as possible. The presentation can wait."

This was one of the finest acts of leadership Meghann had ever witnessed. It was clear to her that Andrea truly prioritizes people ahead of everything else. Almost in disbelief at the compassion she received from Andrea, Meghann jumped on a plane the following morning.

Soon after arriving in New Jersey, it became clear that Dadad was declining quickly, and he could sense it. He wanted to go home. Although it wasn't easy, Meghann's family was able to get Dadad discharged so he could receive hospice care at his house.

Being home renewed Dadad's spirits. He seemed to be doing very well at first. But a few days later, his breathing suddenly started to change. It became clear that he would not live for months. He was almost ready to let go.

Meghann sat by her Dadad and stroked his face and hands. She asked, "Are you afraid?"

"No," he replied.

"Do you know that you are loved by so many?" she asked.

"Yes," he said.

Other family members shared their final loving words with him as well. Dadad requested that those present call a few other family members and ask them to come see him. When each person arrived, Dadad would look at them and say something to acknowledge them. Among the most touching was, "I waited for you."

Surrounded by those he loved, and who loved him, Dadad was at peace. He even joked a bit. At one point, while others were discussing baseball, he said something like, "I want to go there."

Meghann's grandmother, Dadad's beloved wife for nearly sixty years, replied, "Where, George, to a ball game?"

"No," he replied, "to be with my mom and dad."

His wife tensed with sadness and gasped a bit when she heard those words.

"Or . . . maybe not," he said, as everyone laughed.

Not long after, around 9 PM, Meghann thought Dadad had let go when his breathing stopped. But a cherished family friend and neighbor, who is a nurse, said that he still had a heartbeat. She said that Dadad could likely still hear everyone and was fighting to hold on because of that. A few minutes later, as the family quieted and calmed, his heartbeat stopped.

Sadly, I have heard stories of employees being asked to work on the same day a loved one dies, or the same day as the funeral. Meghann was fortunate. Thanks to the kindness and compassion of her manager, Andrea, Meghann was able to be with her Dadad for some of the most important moments of their lives.

Making the Intangible, Tangible

Of all the needs people have for thriving at work, feeling cared for by one's manager may be the most important. Feeling cared for by others is listed right above food, water, and physical safety in Maslow's hierarchy of needs. And, according to the Gallup organization, a caring manager may be the need most strongly correlated with employee engagement.

When team members feel cared for by their managers, they are more likely to feel safe, which enhances creativity and innovation. They are also more likely to go the extra mile and give discretionary effort. And, when team members feel cared for by their managers, they're more likely to give a manager the benefit of the doubt and forgive mistakes.

Despite it being such an important need to meet, many leaders struggle to develop a practical approach to better meeting this need. It seems to be the softest of "soft skills," and one that is hard to define, much less measure. However, I believe it's possible to do both.

We can be fairly certain that a team member feels adequately cared for by her manager when she believes that her manager cares as much as or more about her as a person than the manager cares about what she produces for the team or organization in the short term. There's no doubt that Meghann Dawson felt cared for by Andrea Naef when Andrea demonstrated with her actions that allowing Meghann to spend time with her grandfather was more important than delivering the presentation to the senior leadership team on time.

When I asked Andrea about her approach to leadership, this is almost exactly what she told me. She said, "I don't believe in work-life balance. I believe in life-work balance. I know that if I put people and their lives first, it's both a more rewarding and more effective way to lead."

Many leaders, even those who want to care, often resist the idea that we should care more about team members as people than we do about how much those team members produce. This is usually because they think it means that performing well and feeling cared for are separate needs. But the most caring leaders are deeply concerned about performance. It's just that the motivation caring leaders have for helping team members perform is genuinely caring about the person and wanting them to succeed, not the selfish desire for achievement, promotion, status, or pay raises.

Caring more about a team member as a person than we do about what they produce doesn't mean that we don't hold people accountable to high standards of excellence. Quite the contrary. What it does mean is that whenever we have to choose between hitting a short-term goal and the well-being of a team member, we should choose the latter as often as possible.

Every time we choose to sacrifice the well-being of team members for the sake of our own short-term needs, or those of the team or organization, we send the message that we don't truly care about team members. And every time that message is reinforced, team members' levels of engagement, trust, and loyalty decline. If that message is reinforced often enough, the team will eventually fail.

However, every time we choose correctly, as Andrea Naef did, and we put people first, we solidify the belief in the mind of team members that we care as much as or more about them as a person than we do about how much they produce in the short term. Counterintuitively, when team members believe that to be true, they are more likely to be engaged, and to produce much more over the long term, than team members who feel like a commodity.

Three Simple Habits for Demonstrating Care

When discussing the topic of caring more about team members as people than about what they produce in the short term, some leaders are concerned that they won't appear authentic if they say they care because they haven't demonstrated care very well in the past. This is a valid concern. However, this shouldn't be an obstacle.

For leaders in this situation, and all other leaders, there's no need to wait until you *feel* like you care more about people than what they produce in the short term. Just start building a new habit that allows you to more consistently *act* in ways that demonstrate that you care about team members as people. If you simply start *acting* as though you care, people will eventually come to believe that you actually do, and so will you.

I experienced this phenomenon firsthand. By nature, I'm very type A and transactional in my relationships. When I first started working to put people first in the companies I've founded, particularly by giving people time away for family matters, I would get very frustrated by the perceived loss of productivity in the short term. But I forced myself to do it anyway.

Now, after years of practice, I no longer get frustrated at all. In fact, I experience a deep sense of fulfillment when I demonstrate care in this way. This gradual yet significant transformation started with some simple habits.

Fortunately, all of the habits outlined in this book are habits that demonstrate that you care because they are all habits for meeting a universal need people have for thriving at work. And the habit of having regular one-to-one meetings during which you learn more about the unique needs your team members have for thriving is particularly useful for helping them feel that you care about them as much as or more than you do about what they produce in the short term. Thus, if you've begun building one or more of the habits outlined in this book, you're already demonstrating that you care about team members.

Another extremely simple habit to start building is to ask team members to share their values and goals with you. I recommend learning about what's most important to them both professionally and personally, and what their professional and personal goals are for one year, three years, and five years from now. There's a free, downloadable template you can use for this at inspiregreatnessbook.com/goals.

You would ask team members to complete the worksheet, and then meet with them to discuss their goals, and potential ways you could help them meet their goals. If possible, I recommend making this part of your onboarding process for new hires. This is a simple, yet powerful way to demonstrate that you care about team members as people. If you check in with team members about their goals once per quarter or so, and rethink potential ways you can help, this habit becomes much more impactful.

Another habit you can start building to consistently demonstrate that you care more about team members as people than you do about how much they produce in the short term is to use two questions as filters for every decision you make that affects your team members. The questions I recommend are some variation of the following:

Is this what's best for the long-term well-being and growth of the team member (or members) this decision affects?

If not, what will the consequences be of doing what's best for the team member(s)?

These questions are powerful as filters for decisions for a couple of reasons. First, every time you ask them, it forces you to think from the perspective of someone who truly cares more about team members as people than what those team members produce in the short term. The more often you think like this, the more often you'll act as though you truly care about team members.

Also, asking the second question almost always reveals that the consequences of doing what's best for the team member won't be catastrophic. If the consequences of doing what's best for the team member won't be catastrophic, then we should do what's best for the team member, for three reasons.

1. What's Best for the Long-Term Well-Being of the Team Member Is Best for the Organization

First, what's best for the team member in the long term is almost always what's best for the organization in the long term. Other than having to lay people off, I can't think of a single exception to this. Can you?

For instance, letting someone go because their values aren't aligned with the organization's values may cause some short-term pain for both parties, but it's clearly what's best for both over the long term. A person whose values aren't aligned with those around them is going to feel like an outsider, and they will likely act in ways that cause harm for the organization. It's best for both parties to help that team member find a place where they would be a better fit.

Another example is letting someone have time away to care for a family member. If we don't give him time away, he won't be fully present at work and his work will almost certainly suffer. Additionally, by showing that we don't care about him, we're eroding engagement, trust, and loyalty.

Conversely, by allowing the team member to be with his family, and demonstrating that we care more about him than what he produces in the short term, we build trust and loyalty. Additionally, when the team member returns, he'll likely be more engaged than ever, and more likely to do his best work.

2. Sustainable, Long-Term Performance

This brings us to the second reason why we should do what's best for the team member as long as the consequences for doing so aren't catastrophic. By definition, if the consequences aren't catastrophic, it means the team or organization will survive to later accomplish a goal that may be missed in the short term. However, the team will be stronger and more engaged than if people's well-being was sacrificed for a short-term goal.

Caring for people is a long-term investment. Although there may be some short-term setbacks when we put people first, we build much stronger, more engaged teams. This means that, over the long term, the team will perform much better than those teams that sacrifice people's well-being for short-term goals.

3. The Gift of Happiness

The third reason we should do what's best for the team member as long as the consequences for doing so aren't catastrophic is that it's simply the right thing to do. And doing the right thing always feels good in the long run. Demonstrating care in this way makes working as a leader much more fulfilling.

As Andera Naef said when I asked her about why she makes people her top priority, "Seeing that I've made a positive impact on another person is what energizes me the most and brings me the most joy."

Andrea puts people first because it's the right thing to do and because it brings her joy. But for those who feel like they may be starting this journey purely for their own benefit, this shouldn't prevent you from starting. This is what some spiritual teachers call being "wisely selfish." There's nothing wrong with putting people first for your own benefit, or even the long-term benefit of the team or organization.

As long as you're demonstrating with your actions that you care more about team members as people than you do about what they produce in the short term, everybody wins. And the more often you put people first, the sooner your motivation will be genuinely selfless, which will help you to be even more effective at consistently inspiring greatness in your team members.

• • • Action Items for Chapter 16 • • •

1. Please visit inspiregreatnessbook.com/goals and download a copy of the template for learning the goals and values of your team members. Then ask them to complete the worksheet, schedule a time to discuss it with them, and create a calendar event with a reminder for once each quarter to discuss it with them during a one-to-one meeting.

2. Please make the process in step 1 part of your onboarding system.

3. Please type and print out some variation of the two questions below and post them where you can see them so that you can make a habit of using them as filters for decisions.

> Is this what's best for the long-term well-being and growth of the team member (or members) that this decision affects?
>
> If not, what will the consequences be of doing what's best for the team member(s)?

Fostering Belonging

The Power of Meaningful Relationships

I n 1938, as the Great Depression was finally nearing its end, a group of researchers at Harvard University, led by a medical doctor named Clark Heath, launched an ambitious study with the hopes of discovering the most important variables for determining whether or not a person would live a long and happy life.

The plan was to track a group of Harvard students from their sophomore year until the day they died, along with a control group of men from less affluent areas of Boston (Harvard was an all-male school at the time, so both the test group and the control group were made up of only men).

Longitudinal studies like this almost never succeed. They often fall apart after a decade or two because too many participants leave the study, or the researchers run out of funding, or the people running the study leave, or die, and no one fills the void to continue the study. Nevertheless, the team secured funding for their work and began gathering data.

At first, the researchers focused on the prevailing thoughts at the time regarding health and happiness in life, factors such as genetics, physical constitution, intelligence, and personality traits. The team gathered data on skulls, organs, and even handwriting.

Despite the odds, the study survived the turnover of three directors over seventy-five years, and kept enough of the original participants to provide an enormous amount of statistically significant data. The participants in the study experienced incredible variety in how their lives progressed. The men ended up becoming lawyers, bricklayers, factory workers, doctors, and one, John F. Kennedy, the president of the United States. Some became alcoholics. Some became schizophrenics. Some men had incredible stories of going from rags to riches. Others experienced going from the top socioeconomic status to the bottom.

Throughout the study, researchers conducted surveys and in-person interviews to gather as much data as possible about how the men in the study lived their lives. They took video of the men interacting with their wives, and interviewed the men's children. They reviewed medical records and, in the later years of the study, even drew blood to study DNA and used magnetic resonance imaging (MRI) to gather data on physical health and brain function.

About sixty-five years into the study, the director at the time, George Vaillant, presented some early findings on what contributed to a healthy life, which he published in his book *Aging Well*. These factors included physical activity, absence of alcohol abuse and smoking, the ability to cope with life's ups and downs, having a healthy weight, and having a stable marriage.

However, during the last ten years of the study, as nearly all of the participants neared the end of their lives, some very important insights were discovered by the fourth director of the study, Dr. Robert Waldinger, and his team. It became clear that meaningful, caring relationships were the best predictor of both happiness throughout life and even physical health.

As Robert stated in his popular TED Talk,

We've learned . . . that social connections are really good for us, and that loneliness kills. It turns out that people who are more socially connected to family, to friends, to community, are happier, they're physically healthier, and they live longer than people who are less well connected.

And the experience of loneliness turns out to be toxic. People who are more isolated than they want to be from others find that they are less happy, their health declines earlier in midlife, their brain functioning declines sooner, and they live shorter lives than people who are not lonely.

How Meaningful Relationships Drive Business Results

I first met Robert Waldinger at a leadership conference put on by the American Society of Association Executives (ASAE), where we were both keynote speakers. When I chatted with Robert during a social event at the conference, he mentioned that, despite the popularity of his TED Talk (it had about ten million views at the time), he was not invited to speak at business meetings or conferences as frequently as other TED speakers with less popular talks.

It seems that many people in the business world haven't made the connection between meaningful, caring relationships at work and improved business outcomes. However, such a connection certainly exists. In fact, having meaningful, caring relationships with peers at work may be the most important driver of employee engagement after feeling cared for by one's manager.

There is an abundance of evidence for the fact that meaningful, caring relationships help improve team performance, including anecdotal evidence, common sense, and a large body of empirical evidence.

As the Harvard Study of Adult Development—which was the most robust longitudinal study ever conducted—found, the most important universal need for human thriving is meaningful, caring relationships. This applies to thriving at work just as much as it does to life outside the workplace.

The people who work in an organization are human beings. When human beings thrive outside of work, they are much more likely to thrive at work, and vice versa.

Also, human beings evolved as social animals whose very survival depended on caring relationships. Relative to most other predators, humans are very slow and weak. Our strength came from working together in groups. The universal need to feel like we belong to a group is literally hardwired into us for survival.

And, as common sense would dictate, the groups who work together the best are the ones in which individuals have the healthiest relationships with each other. This fact is borne out in decades of research as well.

The best evidence that we truly belong to a group is when other members of the group care about us, and we care about them. According to research from Gallup, teams with people who truly care about each other collaborate better and are more innovative. However, globally, only three out of every ten employees strongly agree that they have a best friend at work. By improving that ratio to six in ten, organizations could realize 28 percent fewer safety incidents, 5 percent higher customer engagement scores, and *10 percent higher profit*.

Gallup also discovered a unique social trend among employees on top-performing teams. According to Gallup, "when employees have a deep sense of affiliation with their team members, they take positive actions that benefit the business that they may not otherwise even consider." It turns out that employees will do more for a person (or people) they care about than they will for an organization.

Thus, by helping team members to meet the universal need of belonging—having meaningful, mutually caring relationships—we are helping them meet what evidence suggests is the most important need for thriving in life. This is an extremely valuable gift to give. And helping team members meet this need is very good for creating a culture of sustainable high performance and driving extraordinary business results.

When I asked Garry Ridge, the former CEO of the WD-40 Company, what he thought was the most important factor for realizing the extraordinary business outcomes the company had realized under his leadership, he responded almost immediately, "It's our culture."

I also asked Garry what was the most important element of the culture. He said that they had created a genuine sense of belonging to a "tribe." I've noticed that when I speak with employees at the WD-40 Company, they don't refer to each other as employees, or team members, or colleagues. In almost every instance, they refer to each other as "tribe members." Tribe members at the WD-40 Company know that nothing is more important than taking care of other members of the tribe. As they would say, "Creating positive lasting memories for tribe members."

There are many, many stories of tribe members demonstrating with their behaviors that the top priority at the WD-40 Company is to take care of fellow tribe members. One example is of a married couple who were both tribe members at the WD-40 Company, whose daughter was diagnosed with brain cancer. Without any direction from senior management, the tribe self-organized to take incredibly good care of this couple and their daughter.

Tribe members organized regular food deliveries so the family wouldn't have to cook while the daughter was going through treatment. They organized fundraisers. And they organized a mechanism to allow other tribe members to donate paid time off (PTO) to the couple so they had as much time as needed to take care of their daughter.

Other tribe members have benefited from this idea as well. Recently, a tribe member needed extra time away to deal with personal issues. The tribe member in charge of organizing PTO donations sent out an email that let the tribe know a fellow member needed help, and would benefit by having a good deal of extra PTO. The request was completely fulfilled almost immediately. Within minutes of sending the email describing the need, the tribe member had to send another email letting people know that no more donations were needed.

Creating the Conditions for Meaningful, Caring Relationships to Form

I am almost always met with resistance when I work with leaders on the topic of helping team members to form meaningful, caring relationships. One of the most common things I hear is, "It's not my job to tell team members they need to be friends." You might have a similar thought when you read about the survey item Gallup uses in its Q12 survey, "I have a best friend at work."

I actually agree. It is not the job of a leader to make people get along, form meaningful relationships, or become friends. However, an extremely important job for a leader is to create the conditions for meaningful, mutually caring relationships to form.

If leaders create the right environment, team members may not all become friends, but they will develop meaningful relationships that include respect for each other, and even caring about each other. And these types of relationships are perhaps the most important element of high-performing teams.

The foundation of meaningful, mutually caring relationships is understanding. When we understand a person, even if the person is someone we don't like very much, we can at least respect that person, and are much more likely to care about that person's well-being and success.

A striking example of this is how Daryl Davis, a renowned black musician, routinely becomes friends with people who hate him when they first meet him. These people hate him not because of some flaw in Daryl's character. They hate him simply because he has dark skin. These people are members of the Ku Klux Klan (KKK).

Daryl first learned about racism in the 1960s, at a young age, when people threw bottles and rocks at him while he marched in a Boy Scout parade. His parents explained to him that some people might hate him just because he has dark skin. Daryl found this very hard to believe and he became fascinated with understanding how people could hate other people without knowing anything about them. Although he would one day make music his profession, his enduring obsession is with race relations.

In the 1980s, during his time playing with a country music band in Maryland, he met and befriended a member of the KKK. Soon after, it occurred to him that meeting with KKK members could be a great way to understand how people become racist. So, he began intentionally setting up meetings with members of the KKK.

Daryl begins the relationship with only one intent, to understand the other person. He asks lots of nonthreatening questions about how a particular KKK member came to have the beliefs he has.

Daryl's intent is not to challenge the beliefs of the KKK member, or to point out the errors in thinking that led to his extreme beliefs. Daryl asks questions with the pure intent of genuinely wanting to understand the KKK member and where he is coming from.

The results of this approach are nothing less than extraordinary. Most of the hundreds of KKK members, and other white supremacists, with whom Daryl has built relationships have become his friends.

Often, these KKK members will be at a KKK meeting on a particular night, speaking of how whites are clearly the superior race and of how the rightful place of blacks is to serve whites. Then, the very next night, these people will have Daryl Davis over to their house for dinner. After developing a longtime relationship with Daryl, one KKK member stated that he has greater respect for Daryl Davis than he does for many of his fellow KKK members.

In most cases, the KKK members with whom Daryl Davis interacts develop such a profound friendship with him that they come to see the blatantly obvious errors in the racist views of the KKK, which they had developed after a lifetime of conditioning. After they become friends with Daryl, a black man, their prejudices fall apart, and they end up giving up their cowardly white robes and leaving the KKK. As of this writing, roughly two hundred KKK members have left the KKK after developing a friendship with Daryl.

It's important to note that the reason Daryl Davis is so effective at developing friendships with KKK members is that he is not trying to convince them to leave the KKK. He meets these people where they're at with the intent of truly understanding them, and thus allowing them to eventually understand him.

At the risk of potentially stating the obvious, if a black man can develop meaningful, mutually caring relationships with people who go into the relationship with genuine hatred for him, it is possible for any of the members on your team to form meaningful, mutually caring relationships by creating the conditions for them to understand each other better.

How to Help Team Members Quickly Form Meaningful, Caring Relationships

Building understanding between two people, and thus building a meaningful, mutually caring relationship, can take years, as it often does for Daryl Davis. However, Daryl usually doesn't see his new friends from the KKK very often. Team members at work see each other, whether virtually or in person, nearly every workday, if not every workday.

This is good news. It means that team members at work can develop meaningful, caring relationships with each other much faster than Daryl Davis can with his KKK friends. And, by applying a simple hack for relationship building, leaders can help team members at work develop meaningful, caring relationships even faster. There are two steps to this approach.

First, leaders should ensure that team members have regular conversations that are not work related. In other words, team members should have regular time to socialize.

If you're like me, you may need to reread this chapter a couple of times as you work to create systems for helping team members develop meaningful relationships. You may need regular reminders for a while that time for socializing is not wasted. It's one of the best investments you can make for having a sustainable high-performance culture. Again, Gallup estimates that by doubling the number of team members who have a best friend at work, the average company could increase profits by *10 percent.*

Second, leaders should help create the space for team members to be a little vulnerable during these regular conversations. If the conversations are superficial, like those about sports and the weather, the connections made tend to be superficial as well, and unlikely to facilitate the growth of meaningful, mutually caring relationships.

In a study called the Experimental Generation of Interpersonal Closeness, researchers Arthur and Elaine Aron found that by making some subtle tweaks to the questions people ask each other, a significant difference in closeness can be established. In his excellent book on teams and culture, *The Culture Code,* author Daniel Coyle provides a sample of the questions asked in the study conducted by the Aron team. When you first read the two sets of questions/prompts below, you'll probably think of them as being pretty similar.

Set 1

- What was the best gift you ever received and why?
- Describe the last pet you owned.
- Where did you go to high school? What was your high school like?
- Who is your favorite actor or actress?

Set 2

- If a crystal ball could tell you the truth about yourself, your life, the future, or anything else, what would you want to know?
- Is there something that you've dreamed of for a long time? Why haven't you done it?
- What is the greatest accomplishment of your life?
- When did you last sing to yourself? Or to someone else?

You might be surprised to learn that people feel approximately 24 percent closer to each other after discussing the questions in Set 2 than after discussing the questions/prompts in Set 1. Set 1 includes superficial questions/prompts that allow people to stay in their comfort zones. Set 2, on the other hand, includes questions that require people to open up and to be a little vulnerable. And it's this vulnerability that allows people to develop true understanding and deeper connections.

Following are the practices we use at the companies I've founded, which our team members love. Although you're certainly welcome to apply these practices on your team, it's also possible that our practices stimulate your creativity and help you come up with a practice that best fits your culture.

Because our teams are 100 percent virtual, I believe it is extremely important for team members to have a meaningful connection with each other every day. By "meaningful," I mean more than just a check-in about work progress. I mean connecting as humans.

Thus, one practice we employ is ensuring our teams have daily team meetings. Although work-related check-ins may be part of the meetings, they don't necessarily need to be if there's nothing that people need to share with the team. However, an opportunity to connect as humans is always on the agenda, and it always happens first.

The method we use to allow people to connect as humans is very simple. Each team member briefly shares one thing that brought them happiness at work in the last twenty-four hours, and one thing that brought them happiness away from work in the last twenty-four hours.

This provides an opportunity for a little bit of vulnerability because people often share something from their private lives. And, of course, it provides team members with an opportunity to learn more about important parts of each other's lives, and deepen their understanding of each other. (On a side note, a nice additional benefit is that team members build the habit of scanning their environments for positive experiences, in both their personal and professional lives, which can dramatically improve gratitude and happiness both at work and away from work.)

Another practice we employ is what we call a "virtual watercooler" discussion, which can be applied for both virtual and in-person discussions. This is an opportunity for team members to connect with one team member every week, one-on-one, but with a little more structure than a typical organic watercooler discussion in an office environment.

First, the meetings are regularly scheduled as part of a rotation, so each team member connects with the other team members an equal number of times in a given quarter or year. We structure our virtual watercooler meetings to include a meaningful conversation prompt to start the conversation. These prompts should initiate sharing that goes beyond superficial topics. You could use some of the questions listed earlier in this chapter, or just do an online search for "meaningful conversation starters."

One person speaks about the prompted topic for five minutes while the other person practices listening deeply without interrupting (this allows team members to develop listening skills along with more meaningful relationships). Then they switch roles for five minutes. Then they have five to ten minutes of free-flowing discussion on whatever they'd like to talk about.

By putting a time limit on the discussion, team members can avoid the issue that often arises during organic, in-person watercooler discussions, when one person wants to keep talking and the other one wants to go back to work. A scheduled meeting with a time limit also ensures a good balance between time spent working to achieve goals and time spent developing meaningful relationships.

After you set up the first few watercooler meetings, you can delegate to a team member who likes to socialize the tasks of maintaining the rotation and assigning the roles of who goes first and who picks the conversation prompt for a given discussion. And the team members who are paired for a given week can schedule the meetings for themselves.

When introducing the structured watercooler meetings to your team members, I recommend explaining that these meetings are an investment in them to allow them to connect as human beings, practice communication skills, and have some fun.

At first, team members may not be very excited about the idea, especially those who are introverted. However, I am very confident that team members will soon come to enjoy the structured watercooler meetings and be grateful that you invest time in allowing them to connect in this way.

During our team meetings on days when people have had watercooler meetings, team members almost always state that the experience that brought them happiness at work during the last twenty-four hours was the watercooler discussion they had with a teammate earlier in the day.

• • • Action Items for Chapter 17 • • •

1. Write out a plan for how you'll allow team members to connect as humans every workday, such as sharing with each other one thing that brought them happiness personally, and one thing that brought them happiness professionally, in the last twenty-four hours.

2. Write out a plan for how you'll create the conditions for regular, structured, meaningful, one-to-one conversations to take place between team members, such as the virtual watercooler.

18

Providing Meaning at Work

The Secret to Creating the Most
Attractive Team Culture Possible

In the late 1930s, John Fox began his college career at the Ohio State University (OSU). But he wanted to join the military as an officer, and OSU did not have a Reserve Officer Training Corps (ROTC) program for black men.

Thus, Fox decided to transfer to a historically black university called Wilberforce University, which had an Army ROTC program run by a highly decorated black World War I veteran named Captain Aaron Fisher. Fox later graduated with a degree in engineering and was commissioned as a second lieutenant on June 13, 1940.

Fox was assigned to the 366th Infantry, an all-black regiment that was formed in World War I. The military remained segregated in World War II because many white leaders presumed that black service members would not be as competent in combat as their white peers. And, as if that were not degrading enough, the all-black units were often commanded by white officers from the Deep South.

Lieutenant Fox did not let racist policies deter him and began his training. Over a period of several years, he spent time in Massachusetts, Indiana, and Virginia, and was trained in artillery and anti-tank tactics.

On March 27, 1944, Fox left Camp Patrick Henry in Virginia, traveling on the USS *General William Mitchell*, to join the front lines with US troops fighting in Italy. He was outgoing and made new friends quickly and easily on the ship, partly due to his skill at playing poker.

After spending a few months training in Morocco and Algeria, Fox arrived in the Po Valley of northern Italy on November 4, where he and the rest of the 366th joined the 92nd Infantry, an all-black division, which became fully assembled on December 9.

A few weeks later, on December 23, Fox moved to the front lines. He had volunteered for a four-day Christmas posting, manning an observation post in the town of Sommocolonia. After a quiet Christmas Day, he awoke early on the morning of December 26 to the sound of gunshots.

Overnight, German soldiers had entered the town under the cover of darkness, dressed in civilian clothes, and began attacking US soldiers at 4:50 AM. This was the first time Fox had ever seen combat.

Italian resistance fighters who were guarding the village overnight began calling for support. But Fox quickly realized that the attacking forces were too close for him to call for artillery because the shells would likely result in US casualties. Another officer fired a mortar barrage instead, which caused the German soldiers to retreat.

But the initial assault was just the beginning, and likely executed mostly for the purpose of gathering intelligence. The German forces had a full-scale attack planned.

Not long after the brief retreat, a large number of German soldiers began attacking the town from two directions. They outnumbered Allied forces by roughly a 3:1 ratio. Reinforcements were sent to help those defending the town, but they ran into an ambush, were bogged down, and eventually retreated.

Within a few hours, Germans were infiltrating the town and closing in on Fox's position. Lieutenant Fox began ordering artillery strikes on the outskirts of the town, knowing that those areas were already overrun by the German soldiers.

As the US soldiers gave up ground and consolidated near Fox's position, he began calling for artillery strikes on positions closer and closer to his own. He then ordered the rest of his men to retreat, and stayed behind to continue guiding the artillery strikes.

When a position Fox requested was dangerously close to his own, the commanding officer of the field artillery brigade, Lieutenant Colonel Robert Ross, protested. He told Fox the shells would be too close. Fox clarified the request and confirmed that was just where he wanted the strike to hit.

Shells landing that close would have made the ground shake violently and would have likely been so loud as to partially damage Fox's eardrums. After such a close barrage, he must have been afraid of what could happen if the shells landed any closer.

At approximately 11 AM, Fox observed the German soldiers continuing to close in and realized that he was almost certainly going to be overrun. All he could do at that point was work to slow the advance of the German soldiers to give US forces more time to retreat to safety. And he couldn't do much to help on his own with only his one rifle and limited ammunition.

Thus, Fox called for another artillery strike. The coordinates he gave for the strike were those of his own position.

Colonel Ross protested again, and asked Fox to confirm the coordinates, stating, "Fox, that will be on you!"

Fox replied, "Fire it! . . . Give them hell!" That was the final communication anyone ever had with Lieutenant Fox.

It turns out that his bravery and self-sacrifice did slow the German advance to allow the Allied forces the opportunity to safely retreat. And, about a week later, US forces were able to once again take control of

Sommocolonia. When they arrived, they found the body of Lieutenant Fox in the rubble, surrounded by approximately one hundred dead German soldiers.

· · · · · ·

Lieutenant John Fox found so much meaning in his work that he was willing to sacrifice his life for it. And this was not a knee-jerk reaction made quickly while he was on autopilot.

Over the course of roughly an hour, he gradually asked for artillery shells to be fired increasingly close to him—despite the terrible and frightening impact this must have had on his body and psyche—before asking for and confirming that his comrades fire directly on his position as he became surrounded.

Anyone familiar with military history knows that, although Lieutenant John Fox was incredibly brave and selfless, his story is not unique. There are many, many stories of service members from all branches of the militaries of countries all over the world who found so much meaning in their work that they very consciously placed themselves in imminent, life-threatening danger for the cause.

In most professions, people rarely, if ever, sacrifice their lives for the cause. Of course, this is partly due to the fact that most people don't work in professions that regularly place them in dangerous situations that create the possibility of serious injury or death. However, it's also partly due to the fact that few people find their work deeply meaningful.

This raises two important questions.

1. Is it possible to create such meaningful work for people—in any profession—that, if the opportunity presented itself, they would sacrifice their lives for the cause?
2. Is this even a worthwhile pursuit?

Let's start with the second question.

The Power of Meaningful Work

One of the most subtle yet powerful universal needs people have for thriving is the need to realize meaning in their lives. Since most adults spend about 40 percent of their waking lives working, realizing meaning at work is a universal need for thriving. The need for meaningful work is so powerful that people would give up a significant amount of pay to do work that adds meaning in their lives.

As part of a study conducted by Shawn Achor and his colleagues, published in the *Harvard Business Review* in 2018, the researchers surveyed 2,285 American professionals, across twenty-six industries and a range of pay levels, company sizes, and demographics. The researchers found that *nine out of ten* employees would trade a percentage of their future lifetime earnings to realize greater meaning at work. The average person surveyed stated they would take a *23 percent reduction in earnings* in order to have a job that was always meaningful.

To put this in perspective, Achor notes, the average person spends 21 percent of their income on housing. Thus, for the average person surveyed in Achor's study, having a job that is always meaningful appears to be more important than having a roof over her head.

Leaders could do a tremendous service for people by creating work that consistently adds meaning in the lives of team members. This would also add tremendous value for the team or organization.

Realizing meaning at work is one of the most powerful drivers of employee engagement. As we have seen with so many military service members, if work is meaningful enough, they'll not only sacrifice income to have the job, they'll sacrifice their lives for the cause.

Unfortunately, according to research from Gallup, it seems that most organizations around the globe are failing to help people realize meaning at work. This finding was similar in Achor's study of US organizations as well. His team found that people today see their work as only about half as meaningful as it could be, and that *only one in twenty* respondents rated their current jobs as providing the most meaningful work they could imagine having.

In the pages that follow, you'll learn how to help your team members realize incredible meaning at work, and potentially see their job as providing the most meaningful work they could imagine having.

A Compelling Purpose

One important component of helping people to realize meaning at work is to connect people's work to the impact your organization is making in the lives of the customers you serve and on the local or global community. I believe that there is lower-hanging fruit for creating meaningful work, which is also simpler to create, so we won't go into great depth on this component, but there are a couple of important details that I think are worthwhile to explore here.

First, any organization, even one that makes or sells something as mundane as nuts and bolts, can uncover a compelling purpose that can inspire team members. A great place to start is with the impact you're making in the lives of the customers you serve. This is commonly referred to as the "mission."

The first step is to ensure that the organization as a whole has a clear and compelling mission statement. While this is ultimately the responsibility of senior leaders, it can be helpful to involve as much of the leadership team as possible in crafting the mission statement for the organization.

But leaders of business units, departments, practice areas, and so on don't need to wait on the C-suite to draft or refine the organization-wide mission. I recommend that these leaders also craft a mission statement for their teams that is more specific to the customers they serve.

The most effective mission statements meet a few simple criteria. First, they're brief and easy to understand. Second, they highlight the impact that's being made on the lives of the customer. Third, they are specific enough to provide direction and to make it simple to measure progress toward achieving the mission.

Unfortunately, many mission statements fail to meet these criteria. Following is a real-life example (although I've changed the name of the company):

ABC Store is in the home improvement business and our goal is to provide the highest level of service, the broadest selection of products and the most competitive prices.

Please take a moment here to pause and see if you can rewrite ABC Store's mission statement so that it is brief, highlights the impact on their customers' lives, and is specific.

Pause Here If You Like for the Exercise

As an example, here's how I would rewrite ABC Store's mission statement:

ABC Store helps people easily make their homes more beautiful and comfortable so they experience less stress and more happiness.

This is brief, it focuses on the impact on the customers, and it's specific enough to provide clear direction for measurement. Team members know they should improve or eliminate any aspect of the buying experience that creates friction for people trying to improve their homes.

The last part is a bonus. The mission could certainly be *ABC Store helps people easily make their homes more beautiful and comfortable*. But when we add in the *so they experience less stress and more happiness* we help our team members connect to a meaningful impact in the lives of customers.

Once you or your leadership team have crafted an effective mission statement, the next step is to help team members connect their work to that mission. There are two steps to this.

First, you need to communicate the mission often, both in writing and verbally. Organizations with high levels of engagement often begin or end every team meeting with a verbal reminder of the mission and vision (we'll cover the vision statement soon).

Second, you need to help team members connect the dots between the work they do every day, and why and how it's important for achieving the mission. This can be done in job descriptions. It could be done in a document that you and your team review each week that lists out the mission and how team members' jobs are connected to that mission. And, it can be done once per quarter in conversations, ideally as part of your regular one-to-one meetings.

Perhaps most importantly, team members need to regularly see (at least once per quarter) examples of customers, whether external or internal, who have been positively impacted by the work of their team. This can be stories shared with them, letters written by the customer, a video message from the customer, or an in-person visit from the customer, which is the most impactful.

Research conducted by Adam Grant found that a brief in-person visit from a customer who took a few minutes to describe how a team helped him, and how that help made an impact on his life, resulted in significant, measurable impacts on a team of inside sales representatives (ISRs). A month after the visit from the customer, the ISRs had on average more than doubled their calls per hour and had achieved average weekly revenue increases of more than 400 percent, from $411.74 to $2,083.52.

An Inspiring Vision of the Future

Once your team has crafted a compelling and effective mission statement, you could take some time connecting the work of team members to the impact the organization is making on the community, or society as a whole. This is commonly referred to as the "vision," because it describes an inspiring vision of the future. A vision statement describes what you'd like the world to look like in the future as a result of accomplishing your mission.

It's perfectly okay, and even encouraged, to shoot for the moon here. The vision doesn't even have to be attainable. In fact, there's something about the idea of working to achieve what seems impossible that can inspire people to do amazing work. A compelling vision can unlock a lot of energy and engagement from your team members.

To provide an example for you, below is the vision for all the organizations I've founded and the mission statement for one of them.

Vision

We envision a world in which all leaders and workplace cultures consistently make a positive impact on the growth and well-being of team members.

We believe that this would create the conditions for a permanent end to poverty, violence, and other unnecessary suffering.

Mission

We help managers and team members build and sustain workplace cultures that drive sustainable high performance, while also making a positive impact on the well-being and growth of the managers, team members, and communities they serve.

You likely noticed that, although the vision seems unattainable, there is a clear connection between accomplishing the mission and our vision for a better future.

Following is another example, which builds on the mission I rewrote for ABC Store above.

We envision a world in which all homeowners are kind to their neighbors.

Again, you can see how accomplishing the mission—*ABC Store helps people easily make their homes more beautiful and comfortable so they experience less stress and more happiness*—would help create a world in which homeowners are less stressed, happier, and more consistently kind to their neighbors.

As with the mission statement, the vision statement for the organization is the responsibility of senior leaders. However, if the vision statement for the organization isn't compelling right now, leaders of departments, business units, practice areas, and so on can certainly craft a vision statement for their teams. In fact, the vision statement crafted for a team may end up being adopted by the organization.

In either case, leaders should take some time, perhaps during an off-site retreat, to reflect deeply on the impact they'd like to make on the community or on society as a whole. If the vision isn't something leaders truly believe in, it won't be of much value to them, or the team or organization.

Once the leadership team has crafted a vision statement, the next step is to help team members connect their work to that vision following the same steps described above for connecting their work to the mission.

The Limits of Mission and Vision Statements

Crafting compelling mission and vision statements, communicating them effectively and often, and connecting the work of each team member to the mission and vision are all very important exercises. I strongly recommend every team and organization do this work.

However, the work related to the mission and vision is a sort of "beginner-level" approach to helping team members realize meaning at work, and there are some limitations to its effectiveness.

One limitation occurs as organizations grow. For small organizations, it's easy for all team members to feel a continuous connection to the mission and vision if the leadership team does the work outlined above.

However, in larger organizations, frontline team members often don't feel connected to the organization's mission and vision. In many cases, sadly, they don't even know what the mission and vision are.

The second reason why the impact of a mission and vision may not be as significant as the impact of what you'll learn in the following pages is that many organizations are producing or selling objectively mundane products or services. It can be hard for team members to truly connect to the mission and vision of the organization if that organization isn't "changing the world," and produces or sells things that aren't "sexy," like nuts and bolts.

The WD-40 Company is an excellent example of this. The WD-40 Company produces and sells a chemical compound that cleans and lubricates metal surfaces. I'm not sure you could find a product or service that is any less "sexy" than that.

However, the WD-40 Company has one of the most meaningful workplace cultures on the planet. The company routinely finds that over 90 percent of its team members are engaged, and nearly 99 percent are proud to tell others that they work at the WD-40 Company.

How have they achieved this?

Creating a Meaningful Workplace Culture

The WD-40 Company has done the work described earlier in this chapter. They have crafted a fairly compelling mission and vision (which they call their "purpose"). They communicate the mission and vision regularly and effectively. They regularly share stories of customers, both external and internal, who have been positively impacted by the work of their team members.

But the WD-40 Company has done something significantly more powerful for helping team members find meaning at work. As you may recall from chapter seventeen, the people who work there have created a culture in which all team members know that nothing is more important than helping other "tribe members" to thrive.

I asked Garry Ridge, the CEO who built the current culture at the WD-40 Company, specifically about this. How large a role do the mission and vision play—as they relate to their products and external customers—in terms of creating meaning for tribe members, versus making it clear that everyone's top priority is to take care of each other? He said that although the mission and vision are clearly an important piece of the puzzle, it is their tribal culture that creates, by far, most of the meaning for team members.

At the WD-40 Company, accomplishing the mission of creating "lasting positive memories" for tribe members is a higher priority than creating lasting positive memories for external customers. Garry and the other leaders know that if leaders and tribe members take great care of each other, they'll be much more likely to take great care of external customers, vendors, the community, and thus the financial sustainability of the company.

There are two reasons why a culture in which the top priority is to take care of each other is almost certainly the best way to create the most meaningful workplace culture possible.

First, creating a culture in which the top priority is to take care of your team members and help them to thrive allows people to realize meaning at work literally every day. Team members don't have to wait weeks or months to see an example of the impact they made at work.

If helping each other, taking care of each other, and even sacrificing for each other is the heart of the culture, every day presents multiple opportunities for finding meaning at work. The conversation team members have over dinner almost certainly includes sharing a fulfilling story of how they helped someone at work that day, or someone helped them.

Second, people are more likely to be engaged in efforts to help people who care about them than for those who do not. This is why the most important driver of employee engagement is feeling that one's manager truly cares about them, and the second is almost certainly feeling that one's team members care about them.

Sacrificing for those who care about you is a much more immediate and compelling cause than sacrificing for an organization, or some other distant cause like a large group of people you know nothing about.

Lieutenant John Fox was likely motivated to go to war by the aspiration to stop Hitler's attempt to destroy the people he hated, and potentially take away the freedoms of European and US citizens. However, a number of the freedoms enjoyed by white US citizens were freedoms Fox's country didn't allow him to enjoy, simply because of the color of his skin. He wasn't even allowed to serve in military units with white service members in them. Fox was almost certainly more motivated by the aspiration to take care of the team members who cared about him than he was a country who didn't consider him to be a full citizen.

If you were to ask a military service member who risked near-certain death in combat to save others why he did it, you likely wouldn't get an answer like, "To defend the US Constitution," as admirable as that may be. The answer you would almost certainly get is, "Because they would have done it for me." In fact, this is the exact answer author Simon Sinek received when he asked a number of heroic US service members why they risked near-certain death in combat to save others.

Could you imagine how meaningful going to work would be if you knew that you'd be willing to sacrifice your life for any one of your team members, and that they would do the same for you?

It is possible to create such a culture. And it starts with you.

It starts by committing to making it your top priority to inspire greatness in your team members by serving as a coach who helps them to thrive—to be happy, great human beings who do great work—and asking your team members to do the same. I recommend that you put your priorities in writing and display them where you and everyone else can be reminded of them daily.

As an example, below are the priorities, in order of importance, for the companies I've founded.

1. Taking great care of each other
2. Taking great care of our customers
3. Taking great care of our vendor partners
4. Taking great care of our community
5. Sustaining our company financially

This written commitment then needs to be followed up with small sacrifices, like taking the time to get to know your team members as people, creating opportunities to share mutual vulnerability, and building habits for consistently meeting the needs your team members have for thriving at work and away from work. Once you are leading by example, you can encourage team members to make taking care of each other their top priority, and recognize and appreciate team members for the small sacrifices they make to help each other.

These little sacrifices made consistently by you and your team members, day after day, month after month, year after year, are what form the foundation of a team culture in which people truly care about each other, and would sacrifice greatly for each other. And, of course, this creates a tremendous opportunity for both you and your teammates to realize incredible meaning at work.

The Most Attractive Workplace Culture Possible

If you commit to creating a team culture in which the top priority is taking great care of each other, a natural side effect is that you'll find yourself, and your team members, talking more about qualities like kindness, compassion, and generosity, and looking for ways to develop those qualities. This, I believe, is the lowest-hanging fruit for creating a deeply meaningful workplace that will attract and retain the most talented people possible.

If you take a moment to reflect, I'm confident you'll agree that, at the end of your life, you'll look back and realize that only one thing truly mattered: how well you loved others.

Somewhere deep inside, each of us knows this is true. This is what life is truly all about. We know that what we accomplished will not matter nearly as much as how we treated people along the way.

But we forget. We get caught up with what seems so important now, with things that are easy to measure, like hitting quarterly revenue targets and completing tasks on our to-do list. As a result, for most of us, developing the most important human qualities, like kindness, compassion, and generosity, is something that is reserved for one hour per week on Sunday mornings.

Thus, by creating a workplace culture in which the top priority is inspiring greatness in others—including developing qualities like kindness, compassion, and generosity, and practicing those qualities with team members—you can create the most meaningful workplace possible. You can create a workplace culture that helps people meet the most important need there is in life: the need to love and be loved.

The love I'm referring to is not a feeling and has nothing to do with romance. Love is an action. It's a verb. When we love a person, it means we extend ourselves, and perhaps even sacrifice a bit, to help the other person thrive. This love can be systematically developed in a team or organization to create a workplace culture in which people can experience love, and being loved, on a daily basis.

If you succeed in creating such a workplace culture, you will have the most ideal workplace culture possible, one that will attract and retain the most talented people in the world. You will not only achieve extraordinary business outcomes; you'll be developing amazing human beings—people who make the world a better place simply through their interactions with others—along the way.

You may very well change the world.

Can you imagine a world full of organizations like this, that help their team members to thrive and to bring more kindness, compassion, and generosity into their interactions with others? Can you imagine the positive impacts this would have on our planet and all the people living on it?

I can. I reflect on this every single day.

I hope you'll join me, both in reflecting on this daily, and taking action every day to help you and the other leaders in your organization build the habits for consistently inspiring true greatness in your team members.

• • • Action Items for Chapter 18 • • •

1. Please schedule a time for you and the other leaders on your team to write out, or reevaluate, your mission and vision statements, per the guidance in this chapter, and write out a plan for ensuring that all team members hear and read the mission and vision statements at least once each week.

2. Please schedule a thirty-minute event on your calendar to create a plan for how you'll collect and share (at least once per quarter) examples of how team members are making a positive impact in the lives of internal or external customers, whether these examples are letters written by the customer, a video of the customer sharing about the impact, or inviting the customer to speak to the team directly (this is the most impactful).

3. Right now, please take fifteen minutes to write out what you'd like the top priorities to be for your team or organization, and create a plan for how you'll consistently live those priorities, share them with your team, and recognize and appreciate team members who extend themselves to help other team members.

APPENDIX

A Guide for Using Employee Surveys in a Way That Actually Improves Employee Engagement

I n chapter three, I recommended that leaders and/or HR / people ops teams refrain from using large annual surveys, and instead use twice-monthly surveys—with only one or two questions on them—to get feedback on how well direct managers are meeting the fourteen universal needs that decades of research suggest are most correlated with employee engagement, and that those surveys be tightly synchronized with bite-size training for direct managers.

Often, when leaders first hear about this, they are very excited and see how much more effective this approach is, but they are concerned about how they're going to get a measure of the current level of employee engagement, get open-ended feedback, or get feedback on organization-wide issues. Or they are committed to using an annual survey of some type to qualify for some type of "great place to work" award.

In this appendix, I'll address each of these questions in turn. However, to start, it's important to note that twice-monthly surveys—synchronized with bite-size training for leaders—are not mutually exclusive with other types of surveys. Even more important to note is that you can dramatically improve employee engagement by building a foundation with short, frequent surveys that are responded to in a matter of days with meaningful action, which is why I strongly recommend using only those surveys for at least six months before using any others.

Measuring Progress and Getting a Snapshot of the Level of Employee Engagement

If you use short, twice-monthly surveys synchronized with bite-size training for leaders as part of an ongoing effort to continuously improve employee engagement—which is the approach I highly recommend—you can measure progress in two ways. First, you can measure progress from year to year for each leader who is receiving feedback, and create a rolling measure of employee engagement based on an average of all the different surveys. Second, you can use quarterly pulse surveys to get a sense of employee engagement levels at both the leader and organization level.

For the pulse, I recommend using just three questions to gauge the following:

1. Does the employee's direct manager care about the employee as a person?
2. Is the employee's direct manager helping the employee to grow?
3. Does coming to work make the employee's life more meaningful?

The main reason I recommend just three questions for the pulse survey—and particularly some variation of the three questions above—is that this will allow you to get the data you need to understand the current level of employee engagement without running the risk, inherent with large surveys, of asking for feedback and then not taking action on the feedback quickly enough. The three areas covered above are excellent proxies for a full employee engagement survey. And, since all three of these areas are addressed often with training for direct managers, as described in the approach you learned in Part 1, employees won't have to wait long to see meaningful action being taken in response to their feedback.

Open-Ended Feedback and Organization-Wide Issues

After using short, twice-monthly surveys for six months to build the virtuous cycle of employees giving feedback, feeling heard, and seeing meaningful action being taken in response to their feedback within a matter of days, you could start asking for open-ended feedback and/ or feedback on organization-wide issues. You will have increased the levels of trust and confidence team members have in the leadership team. You will thus likely get higher response rates to your surveys and better feedback.

However, before you deploy any open-ended feedback surveys or organization-wide-issue surveys, I recommend having a solid plan for how you're going to respond to the feedback and show meaningful action in response to it as quickly as possible. Thus, you won't erode the trust and confidence you've built in the previous six months.

Your leadership team might not be able to respond with meaningful action to these types of surveys in a matter of days, but they should be able to respond in a couple weeks. In order to achieve this speedy response, I recommend the following.

First, do not deploy a survey unless any leaders who would need to be involved in addressing an issue discovered with a survey have blocked off time on their calendars to meet and discuss potential solutions within a few days of the survey closing. If this is not done far enough in advance, it can be very hard to coordinate schedules quickly enough to enable a speedy response. There should be enough time scheduled for leaders to create one or more action plans for responding to the issue discovered, which they should then share with employees, along with the proposed timeline for resolving the issue, immediately after the meeting.

This first step may sound challenging, but it is well worth the time and effort. Remember, research from Gallup has found that employee engagement is nearly three times higher in organizations when employees strongly agree with the statement *My organization acts upon the results of surveys I complete.*

Second, only ask one, highly focused question at a time on surveys for open-ended feedback or feedback on organization-wide issues. For instance, an open-ended question might be, *What is one thing the senior leadership team should do more of to increase the levels of confidence you have in them?* By asking only one question and for only one response, it helps you know who should be in the meeting to discuss the response, and makes it easier for those leaders to find patterns in the feedback and a good potential action plan for addressing it.

Integrating the Approach You Learned in This Book with Annual Surveys

If you're in an organization that has just done an annual survey, or have already committed to doing one, or plan on continuing to do them for the purposes of qualifying for some type of "great place to work" award, you might have been alarmed after reading Part 1. You may have realized just how ineffective these types of surveys often are for improving employee engagement, or how they can often actually reduce employee engagement.

There is good news for you, though. It is possible to integrate the approach you learned in Part 1 with large annual surveys to help ensure that the large annual surveys don't have as much of a negative impact on employee engagement. Let's start with the case of just having completed an annual survey, or knowing that you're committed to one soon.

For Those Who Just Completed an Annual Survey, or Who Are About to Complete One

First, I recommend looking at all the questions on the survey and dividing them into areas that can be addressed by direct managers and those that are organization-wide issues.

Then, for the areas that can be addressed by direct managers, find the six questions with the lowest scores and provide training for the direct managers that addresses one behavior every two weeks for twelve weeks, following the guidance in chapter four. If you're creating the training in house, you just need to create one every two weeks to stay ahead of the leaders being trained. This approach will allow your leaders to start demonstrating meaningful action in response to employee feedback as quickly as possible.

Next, start scheduling monthly meetings with the leaders best suited to address the organization-wide questions, starting with the lowest scores first. This will allow employees to see action being taken within thirty days on at least one organization-wide issue.

After twelve weeks, employees will probably have forgotten about the annual survey, so you could start utilizing the approach you learned in Part 1, with twice-monthly surveys synchronized with training for leaders.

For Those Who Plan on Using Annual Surveys for "Great Place to Work" Awards

If you plan on using annual surveys to qualify for "great place to work" awards, and you have at least a quarter before the next survey, you could start deploying the approach described in Part 1 now. Then, before deploying the annual survey, you could be completely transparent about the purpose of the annual survey—that is, to see if you qualify for a "great place to work" award—and let employees know that you may not respond to all of the feedback from that survey immediately. But, as they've seen recently, you'll be continuously asking for and responding to feedback throughout the year.

For People Who'd Like Help with Utilizing Surveys in a Way That Improves Employee Engagement

If you think it would be helpful, I would be happy to schedule a free, forty-five-minute consultation with you to discuss how to create a winning survey solution based on your unique situation. Just visit inspiregreatness book.com/surveys to learn more and schedule a free consultation.

ACKNOWLEDGMENTS

The list of people I'd like to thank for helping make this book a reality is long. In a way, almost everyone I know has contributed to this book in some way.

In the interest of not using up too much more paper, however, I'm going to keep these acknowledgments brief by focusing on those people in my life who contributed the most, and the most recently, to this book.

I'd like to thank my wife, Leah, for being an early reader of the manuscript, and for providing both validation of the overall book and very helpful feedback for making it better.

I'd like to thank my children, Chiara and Francisco, for being such helpful coaches and improving my ability to identify and meet the legitimate needs people have for thriving.

I'd like to thank all of the guests I have interviewed on the *Business Leadership Today* podcast, with a special thanks to Bruce Tulgan, Shane Green, and Mike Figliuolo. Your interviews helped sharpen and refine some of the key discoveries that led to the writing of this book.

I'd like to thank my publisher, Matt Holt, who, for reasons I'm still not sure of, has believed in me and my potential for making a significant, positive impact on our society, since the first time we met. Thank you for taking a chance on me with my first book, when you were at Wiley. And thank you for so quickly and confidently saying "Yes" to this project. Your confidence in me has helped me immensely, particularly in terms of believing in myself, which has inspired me to work even harder to serve others.

I'd like to thank my agent, Michael Palgon, for being so involved after the book deal and making this book the best book it can be. Your suggestions helped improve this book significantly.

I'd like to thank my senior editor, Katie Dickman. You offered just the right balance of enthusiastic affirmation, which helped me believe that this could become a great book (hopefully we've achieved that), and very helpful feedback on how to improve it.

I'd like to thank my copy editor, Michael Fedison. You did an amazing job of making so many parts of this book more clear and concise, and thus easier and more enjoyable to read. You are very good at what you do!

I'd like to thank my friend and colleague Joe Calloway for providing the early validation of the approach that led to this book, which inspired me to work even harder to share this approach with as many organizations as possible.

I'd also like to thank you, the reader, for taking the time to read this book. If you apply even a little of what you learned here, you will make a positive impact in the lives of your team members, the people in their lives, and the people in those people's lives, and so on. Thus, the actions you take to inspire greatness in your team members will be a gift to many, many people. For this, I'm very, very grateful. Thank you again!

NOTES

Chapter 1

7   *Jennifer is a young*   Names and other details of this story were changed, for the purpose of anonymity.

8   *She knew that after*   McFeely, Shane, and Ben Wigert. 2019. "This Fixable Problem Costs U.S. Businesses $1 Trillion." Gallup. March 13, 2019. https://www .gallup.com/workplace/247391/fixable-problem-costs-businesses-trillion.aspx.

8   *According to the authors*   Sull, Donald, Charles Sull, and Ben Zweig. 2022. "Toxic Culture Is Driving the Great Resignation." *MIT Sloan Management Review*. January 11, 2022. https://sloanreview.mit.edu/article/toxic-culture-is -driving-the-great-resignation/.

10   *Below are just a*   Sorenson, Susan. 2013. "How Employee Engagement Drives Growth." Gallup. January 7, 2023. https://www.gallup.com/workplace/236927 /employee-engagement-drives-growth.aspx.

11   *Gallup estimates that low*   Pendell, Ryan. 2022. "The World's $7.8 Trillion Workplace Problem." Gallup. June 14, 2022. https://www.gallup.com/workplace /393497/world-trillion-workplace-problem.aspx.

11   *Employee engagement has been*   Blacksmith, Nikki, and Jim Harter. 2011. "Majority of American Workers Not Engaged in Their Jobs." Gallup. October 28, 2011. https://news.gallup.com/poll/150383/majority-american-workers-not -engaged-jobs.aspx.

12   *As of this writing in 2023*   Harter, Jim. 2023. "U.S. Employee Engagement Needs a Rebound in 2023." Gallup. January 25, 2023. https://www.gallup.com /workplace/468233/employee-engagement-needs-rebound-2023.aspx.

12   *However, according to research*   Beck, Randall, and Jim Harter. 2015. "Managers Account for 70% of Variance in Employee Engagement." Gallup. April 21, 2015.

https://news.gallup.com/businessjournal/182792/managers-account-variance
-employee-engagement.aspx.

13   *Unfortunately, even when leadership*   Todd, Alan, and Robert E. Quinn. "Your
Leadership Training Is Probably a Waste of Money. Here's What's Missing."
Entrepreneur. July 26, 2018. https://www.entrepreneur.com/leadership/your
-leadership-training-is-probably-a-waste-of-money/317137; Brinkerhoff, Robert O. *Telling Training's Story: Evaluation Made Simple, Credible, and Effective.*
San Francisco: Berrett-Koehler Publishers, 2006; HBS Working Knowledge.
n.d. "Companies Waste Billions of Dollars on Ineffective Corporate Training."
Forbes. July 25, 2016. https://www.forbes.com/sites/hbsworkingknowledge/2016
/07/25/companies-waste-billions-of-dollars-on-ineffective-corporate-training
/?sh=7a7f19eb4d22.

14   *Ana is one of*   The names in this story were changed for the purpose of anonymity.

Chapter 2

19   *One study, for instance*   Keck, Madeleine. 2022. "Australian Men Rank Among
Most Misogynistic in Western World: Report." *Global Citizen.* March 15, 2022.
https://www.globalcitizen.org/en/content/australian-men-rank-among-most
-misogynistic/.

21   *On one occasion, early*   Cranston, Matthew. 2022. "The Little-Known Aussie
Behind One of the World's Top Brands." *Australian Financial Review.* August
12, 2022. https://www.afr.com/world/north-america/the-aussie-stepping-down
-as-ceo-of-a-brand-everyone-knows-20220725-p5b46g.

23   *In a groundbreaking study*   Kotter, J. P., and J. L. Heskett. *Corporate Culture and
Performance.* New York: Free Press, 1992.

27   *Research suggests that, thanks*   Markowsky, George. *Encyclopædia Britan-
nica.* "Information Theory—Physiology." 2019. https://www.britannica
.com/science/information-theory/Physiology; "Module 4: Implicit Bias &
Microaggressions—Project READY: Reimagining Equity & Access for
Diverse Youth." n.d. Accessed May 22, 2023. https://ready.web.unc.edu/section
-1-foundations/module-4-implicit-bias-microaggressions/#:~:text=In%20fact
%2C%20scientific%20research%20shows.

27   *Some researchers believe that*   Hass, Daniel. 2015. "This Is How the Brain Filters
Out Unimportant Details." *Psychology Today.* February 11, 2015. https://www
.psychologytoday.com/us/blog/brain-babble/201502/is-how-the-brain-filters
-out-unimportant-details; Ortega, Rodrigo, Vladimir López, Ximena Car-
rasco, María Josefina Escobar, Adolfo M. García, Mario A. Parra, and Francisco
Aboitiz. 2020. "Neurocognitive Mechanisms Underlying Working Memory
Encoding and Retrieval in Attention-Deficit/Hyperactivity Disorder." *Scientific
Reports* 10 (1): 7771. https://doi.org/10.1038/s41598-020-64678-x.

Chapter 3

39   *Research from Dr. Tasha Eurich*   Eurich, Tasha. *Insight: The Surprising Truth About How Others See Us, How We See Ourselves, and Why the Answers Matter More Than We Think.* New York: Currency, 2018.

43   *Research published by Shawn Achor*   Achor, Shawn, Andrew Reece, Gabriella Kellerman, and Alexi Robichaux. 2018. "9 out of 10 People Are Willing to Earn Less Money to Do More-Meaningful Work." *Harvard Business Review.* November 6, 2018. https://hbr.org/2018/11/9-out-of-10-people-are-willing-to-earn -less-money-to-do-more-meaningful-work.

44   *When you ask questions*   Gallup Inc. "How to Improve Employee Engagement in the Workplace." Gallup. 2020. https://www.gallup.com/workplace/285674 /improve-employee-engagement-workplace.aspx; Wood, Jade, and Bailey Nelson. "The Manager's Role in Employee Well-Being." Gallup. November 29, 2017. https://www.gallup.com/workplace/236249/manager-role-employee.aspx.

Chapter 4

45   *From 2004 to 2006*   Licata, Lauren. "Mark Roberge Shares His Story About Taking Hubspot from a Class Project in 2005 to 80M in Revenue in 2013." Built in Chicago. February 24, 2014. https://www.builtinchicago.org/blog/exclusive -interview-hubspot-s-mark-roberge-talks-startups-growing-sales-teams-and -future-crm-so; Roberge, Mark. *The Sales Acceleration Formula: Using Data, Technology, and Inbound Selling to Go from $0 to $100 Million.* Hoboken, NJ: Wiley, 2015; Bazar, Cece. "Building a Generational Software Company— Insights from HubSpot's CRO Mark Roberge." *OpenView.* April 12, 2016. https://openviewpartners.com/blog/building-a-generational-software-company -insights-from-hubspots-cro-mark-roberge/; Ughade, Nupura. "What to Expect When You Scale: Lessons from Mark Roberge." *Chargebee Blog.* September 14, 2020. https://www.chargebee.com/blog/scaling-lessons-mark-roberge/; "Mark Roberge | Building a Scalable, Predictable Sales Machine." Stern Strategy Group: Speaking & Advisory and PR. April 10, 2020. Video, https://www .youtube.com/watch?v=9H5DO9KAtw0.

57   *Research from Gallup has found that engagement*   Clifton, Jim, James K. Harter, and Gallup Inc. *It's the Manager: Gallup Finds the Quality of Managers and Team Leaders Is the Single Biggest Factor in Your Organization's Long-Term Success.* New York: Gallup Press, 2019.

58   *According to the most recent*   Assuming the average engagement level for the top quartile is 70 percent of employees engaged (it's lower than that, since Gallup states that the top thirty-eight companies in the world measure an average of 71 percent engagement, making this a conservative estimate), and the average

engagement level for the bottom quartile is 15 percent (it's probably higher, since the average of all US companies is 32 percent, making this a conservative estimate), this means there is a difference of 55 percentage points between the top-quartile companies and the bottom quartile. Since companies in the top quartile of employee engagement levels have 18 percent higher sales than those in the bottom quartile, one could estimate that for every one employee out of one hundred that moved from not engaged (or actively disengaged) to engaged, a company would realize a 0.33 percent increase in revenue. Sorenson, Susan. 2013. "How Employee Engagement Drives Growth." Gallup. June 20, 2013 (updated January 7, 2023). https://www.gallup.com/workplace/236927 /employee-engagement-drives-growth.aspx.

58   *Thus, even if the*   Clifton, Jim, James K. Harter, and Gallup Inc. *It's the Manager: Gallup Finds the Quality of Managers and Team Leaders Is the Single Biggest Factor in Your Organization's Long-Term Success.* New York: Gallup Press, 2019.

Chapter 5

72   *Tara, Aaron's colleague, had*   For the purpose of anonymity, Tara is not her real name.

74   *There is, however, an*   Garnett, Laura. 2020. "Is Your Environment Hurting Your Chances for Success?" Inc.com. February 6, 2020. https://www.inc.com/laura -garnett/is-your-environment-hurting-your-chances-at-success.html; Fabian, Renee. 2017. "The Psychology Behind Success and Failure | Talkspace." Talkspace. October 11, 2017. https://www.talkspace.com/blog/psychology-behind -success-failure/; Brockhaus, Robert H. 1980. "Psychological and Environmental Factors Which Distinguish the Successful from the Unsuccessful Entrepreneur: A Longitudinal Study." *Academy of Management Proceedings.* 1980 (1): 368–72. https://doi.org/10.5465/ambpp.1980.4977943.

Chapter 6

85   *According to Gallup, globally*   Gallup Inc. n.d. "How to Measure Employee Engagement with the Q12." Gallup. https://www.gallup.com/workplace/356045 /q12-question-summary.aspx.

89   *As my colleague Shane*   "Shane Green on Creating a High-Performance Culture." *Business Leadership Today.* November 29, 2021. Podcast, website, 1:02:55. https:// businessleadershiptoday.com/shane-green-on-creating-a-high-performance -culture/.

Chapter 7

93   *During the Christmas season*   kibitzor. 2023. "Trader Joe's did something awesome!" *Reddit.* Accessed May 22, 2023.https://www.reddit.com/r/reddit.com/comments/agsb4/trader_joes_did_something_awesome/.

94   *The reason that leaders*   "Inside Trader Joe's Podcast: Episode 2 | It's About Values." n.d. www.youtube.com. Accessed June 26, 2023. https://www.youtube.com/watch?v=z55DHaGyNTM.

95   *According to Gallup, by*   Gallup Inc. n.d. "How to Measure Employee Engagement with the Q12." Gallup. https://www.gallup.com/workplace/356045/q12-question-summary.aspx.

Chapter 8

108   *In 2019, the United Nations*   2019. "Stress, Overtime, Disease, Contribute to 2.8 Million Workers' Deaths per Year, Reports UN Labour Agency." *UN News.* April 18, 2019. https://news.un.org/en/story/2019/04/1036851.

108   *Jeffrey Pfeffer, a professor*   Miller, Kara. 2022. "Workplace Stress Is Making Us Sick. Can We Hold Bosses Responsible?" *Boston Globe.* April, 25, 2022. https://www.bostonglobe.com/2022/04/25/business/workplace-stress-is-making-us-sick-can-we-hold-bosses-responsible/.

110   *There's also a large*   Carmichael, Sarah Green. 2015. "The Research Is Clear: Long Hours Backfire for People and for Companies." *Harvard Business Review.* August 19, 2015. https://hbr.org/2015/08/the-research-is-clear-long-hours-backfire-for-people-and-for-companies.

110   *For instance, Erin Reid*   Reid, Erin. 2015. "Why Some Men Pretend to Work 80-Hour Weeks." *Harvard Business Review.* April 28, 2015. https://hbr.org/2015/04/why-some-men-pretend-to-work-80-hour-weeks.

Chapter 9

117   *Lieutenant Colonel (LTC) Julio Acosta*   The names in this story were changed for the purpose of anonymity.

119   *However, research from Gallup has also*   Gallup Inc. n.d. "How to Measure Employee Engagement with the Q12." Gallup. https://www.gallup.com/workplace/356045/q12-question-summary.aspx.

120   *W. Edwards Deming, the late*   Scholtes, Peter R., David L. Bayless, Gabriel A. Massaro, Nancy K. Roche, and Brian L. Joiner. *The Team Handbook for Educators: How to Use Teams to Improve Quality.* Madison, WI: Joiner Associates, 1994.

Chapter 10

123   *Ricky, as he was*   Branson, Richard. 2018. "The Value of Dyslexic Thinking." Virgin, October 15, 2018. https://www.virgin.com/branson-family/richard-branson-blog/the-value-of-dyslexic-thinking; Branson, Richard. *Losing My Virginity: How I Survived, Had Fun, and Made a Fortune Doing Business My Way.* Updated ed. New York: Crown Business, 2011.

126   *Being "in the zone"*   Oppland, Mike. 2016. "8 Ways to Create Flow According to Mihaly Csikszentmihalyi [+TED Talk]." PositivePsychology.com. December 12, 2016. https://positivepsychology.com/mihaly-csikszentmihalyi-father-of-flow/; Csikszentmihalyi, Mihaly. *Flow: The Psychology of Optimal Experience*, First Harper Perennial Modern Classics ed. New York: Harper Perennial, 2008; Koehn, S., T. Morris, and A. P. Watt. 2013. "Flow State in Self-Paced and Externally-Paced Performance Contexts: An Examination of the Flow Model." *Psychology of Sport & Exercise* 14 (6): 787–795; Nakamura, J., and M. Csikszentmihalyi. 2009. "Flow Theory and Research." In C. R. Snyder & S. J. Lopez (eds.), *Handbook of Positive Psychology*, 195–206. Oxford University Press; Ullén, F., Ö de Manzano, R. Almeida, P. K. Magnusson, N. L. Pedersen, J. Nakamura, and G. Madison. 2012. "Proneness for Psychological Flow in Everyday Life: Associations with Personality and Intelligence." *Personality and Individual Differences* 52 (2): 167–172.

127   *According to research from the Gallup organization*   Gallup Inc. n.d. "How to Measure Employee Engagement with the Q12." Gallup. https://www.gallup.com/workplace/356045/q12-question-summary.aspx.

Chapter 11

131   *Karin Hurt had spent*   Hurt, Karin. 2021. "Building an Innovative, High-Performance Culture." *Business Leadership Today.* October 14, 2021. https://businessleadershiptoday.com/karin-hurt-innovative-high-performance-culture/; Hurt, Karin, and David Dye. *Courageous Cultures: How to Build Teams of Micro-Innovators, Problem Solvers, and Customer Advocates.* New York: HarperCollins Leadership, 2020.

137   *According to a global study*   Marcroft, Darlene. 2021. "A Silenced Workforce: Four in Five Employees Feel Colleagues Aren't Heard Equally, Says Research from the Workforce Institute at UKG." UKG. June 22, 2021. https://www.ukg.com/about-us/newsroom/silenced-workforce-four-five-employees-feel-colleagues-arent-heard-equally-says.

138   *Diverse teams have been shown* Baumgartner, Jeffrey. 2010. "Why Diversity Is the Mother of Creativity." Innovation Management. November 24, 2010. https://innovationmanagement.se/2010/11/24/why-diversity-is-the-mother-of -creativity/; Hewlett, Sylvia Ann, Melinda Marshall, and Laura Sherbin. 2013. "How Diversity Can Drive Innovation." *Harvard Business Review*. December 2013. https://hbr.org/2013/12/how-diversity-can-drive-innovation.

Chapter 12

143   *Studies suggest that 60* Lipman, Victor. n.d. "65% of Employees Want More Feedback (So Why Don't They Get It?)." *Forbes*. Accessed May 22, 2023. https:// www.forbes.com/sites/victorlipman/2016/08/08/65-of-employees-want-more -feedback-so-why-dont-they-get-it/?sh=8976bba914ad; Sorenson, Susan, and Keri Garman. 2013. "How to Tackle U.S. Employees' Stagnating Engagement." Gallup. June 11, 2013. https://news.gallup.com/businessjournal/162953/tackle -employees-stagnating-engagement.aspx; Wigert, Ben, and Nate Dvorak. 2019. "Feedback Is Not Enough." Gallup. May 16, 2019. https://www.gallup.com /workplace/257582/feedback-not-enough.aspx.

144   *The approach of the "feedback sandwich"* Henley, Amy J., and Florence D. DiGennaro Reed. 2015. "Should You Order the Feedback Sandwich? Efficacy of Feedback Sequence and Timing." *Journal of Organizational Behavior Management* 35 (3–4): 321–35. https://doi.org/10.1080/01608061.2015.1093057.

145   *Gallup research has also found* Wigert, Ben, and Nate Dvorak. 2019. "Feedback Is Not Enough." Gallup. May 16, 2019. https://www.gallup.com/workplace /257582/feedback-not-enough.aspx.

145   *Research suggests that one-way* Ibid.

146   *Even better, if you can* Yeager, David Scott, Valerie Purdie-Vaughns, Julio Garcia, Nancy Apfel, Patti Brzustoski, Allison Master, William T. Hessert, Matthew E. Williams, and Geoffrey L. Cohen. 2014. "Breaking the Cycle of Mistrust: Wise Interventions to Provide Critical Feedback Across the Racial Divide." *Journal of Experimental Psychology: General* 143 (2): 804–24. https://doi .org/10.1037/a0033906.

146   *And it's just one* Coyle, Daniel. *The Culture Code*. Random House New York, 2018.

148   *According to research conducted* Karkara, Noor. 2022. "35 Performance Management Statistics Every HR Leader Should Know." Darwinbox.com. October 11, 2022. https://blog.darwinbox.com/performance-management-statistics#:~:text= Top%2DDown%20vs%20Bottom%2DUp.

Chapter 13

157   *Perhaps the most telling* Semler, Ricardo. 1994. "Why My Former Employees Still Work for Me." *Harvard Business Review*. January 1, 1994. https://hbr
.org/1994/01/why-my-former-employees-still-work-for-me; "Ricardo Semler a Revolutionary Model of Leadership INS517—INS Ricardo Semler: A Revolutionary—Studocu." n.d. Studocu. Accessed May 22, 2023. https://
www.studocu.com/en-us/document/texas-am-university-kingsville/leadership
-change-innovation/ricardo-semler-a-revolutionary-model-of-leadership-ins517
/22566248; Semler, Ricardo. *Maverick: The Success Story Behind the World's Most Unusual Workplace.* 1st trade print ed. New York: Warner Books, 1995.

158   *There is an abundance of evidence linking* Sokol, Bryan, W. Frederick, M. E. Grouzet, and Ulrich Mueller. *Self-Regulation and Autonomy: Social and Developmental Dimensions of Human Conduct.* New York: Cambridge University Press, 2013. https://doi.org/10.1017/CBO9781139152198; Fischer, Ronald, and Diana Boer. 2011. "What Is More Important for National Well-Being: Money or Autonomy? A Meta-Analysis of Well-Being, Burnout, and Anxiety Across 63 Societies." *Journal of Personality and Social Psychology* 101 (1): 164–84. https://doi
.org/10.1037/a0023663; Johannsen, Rebecca, and Paul J. Zak. 2020. "Autonomy Raises Productivity: An Experiment Measuring Neurophysiology." *Frontiers in Psychology* 11 (963): doi:10.3389/fpsyg.2020.00963.

158   *In self-determination theory* Deci, Edward, and Richard Ryan. 2015. "Self-Determination Theory—an Overview | ScienceDirect Topics." Sciencedirect.com. 2015. https://www.sciencedirect.com/topics/social-sciences/self-determination
-theory.

Chapter 14

166   *The research from Gallup has shown* Clifton, Jim, and James K. Harter. *It's the Manager: Moving from Boss to Coach.* New York: Gallup Press, 2019.

167   *Researchers noticed that* Snowdon, D. A. 1997. "Aging and Alzheimer's Disease: Lessons from the Nun Study." *The Gerontologist* 37 (2): 150–56. https://doi.org
/10.1093/geront/37.2.150; Allen, Kate. 2015. "How Nun Dodged Alzheimer's Part of Dementia's Mystery." Star.com (Toronto). November 24, 2015. https://
www.thestar.com/news/world/2015/11/24/how-nun-dodged-alzheimers-part
-of-dementias-mystery.html.

168   *According to Gallup, only one* Gallup Inc. n.d. "How to Measure Employee Engagement with the Q12." *Gallup.* https://www.gallup.com/workplace/356045
/q12-question-summary.aspx.

170   *To be more strategic* Business Leadership Today. "Mike Figliuolo on Building a High-Performance Culture." *Business Leadership Today*, November 11, 2021.

Podcast, website, 31:09. https://businessleadershiptoday.com/mike-figliuolo-on
-building-a-high-performance-culture/.

Chapter 15

178   *According to a report published* Hastwell, Claire. 2019. "The Business Returns on
High-Trust Work Culture." Great Place to Work®, September 12, 2019. https://
www.greatplacetowork.com/resources/blog/the-business-returns-on-high-trust
-work-culture.

181   *As a result, according to research* American Psychological Association. 2014.
"Employee Distrust Is Pervasive in U.S. Workforce." APA. Accessed May 22,
2023. https://www.apa.org/news/press/releases/2014/04/employee-distrust.

182   *Something very similar happened* Parker, James F. *Do the Right Thing: How Dedicated Employees Create Loyal Customers and Large Profits.* Upper Saddle River, N.J:
Wharton School Pub, 2008.

Chapter 16

190   *And, according to the Gallup organization* Gallup Inc. n.d. "How to Improve
Employee Engagement in the Workplace." Gallup. https://www.gallup.com
/workplace/285674/improve-employee-engagement-workplace.aspx#ite-357473.

Chapter 17

198   *It became clear that meaningful* Mineo, Liz. 2017. "Good Genes Are Nice, but
Joy Is Better." *Harvard Gazette.* April 11, 2017. https://news.harvard.edu/gazette
/story/2017/04/over-nearly-80-years-harvard-study-has-been-showing-how-to
-live-a-healthy-and-happy-life/.

198   *As Robert stated* Waldinger, Robert. n.d. "What Makes a Good Life? Lessons from the Longest Study on Happiness." TED Talks. Video, 12:38. https://
www.ted.com/talks/robert_waldinger_what_makes_a_good_life_lessons_from
_the_longest_study_on_happiness/transcript?language=en.

200   *According to Gallup, "when* Gallup Inc. n.d. "How to Measure Employee
Engagement with the Q12." Gallup. https://www.gallup.com/workplace/356045
/q12-question-summary.aspx.

202   *A striking example of* Davis, Daryl. 2017. "Why I, as a Black Man, Attend KKK
Rallies | Daryl Davis | TEDxNaperville." TED Talks. November 2017. Video,
18:53. https://www.ted.com/talks/daryl_davis_why_i_as_a_black_man_attend
_kkk_rallies?language=en; Howard, Russell. 2017. "Daryl Davis on Converting
200 White Supremacists to Leave the KKK." YouTube. Video, 12:34. https://
www.youtube.com/watch?v=HLtp13Rw8Kc; Brown, Dwane. 2017. "NPR

Choice Page." Npr.org. August 20, 2017. https://www.npr.org/2017/08/20/544861933/how-one-man-convinced-200-ku-klux-klan-members-to-give-up-their-robes.

205 *Again, Gallup estimates that* Gallup Inc. n.d. "How to Measure Employee Engagement with the Q12." Gallup. https://www.gallup.com/workplace/356045/q12-question-summary.aspx.

205 *In a study called* Aron, Arthur, Edward Melinat, Elaine N. Aron, Robert Darrin Vallone, and Renee J. Bator. 1997. "The Experimental Generation of Interpersonal Closeness: A Procedure and Some Preliminary Findings." *Personality and Social Psychology Bulletin* 23 (4): 363–77. https://doi.org/10.1177/0146167297234003.

205 *In his excellent book* Coyle, Daniel. *The Culture Code: The Secrets of Highly Successful Groups*, International ed. New York: Bantam Books, 2018.

Chapter 18

209 *In the late 1930s* Ackerman, Cory M. 2021. "'I Did Not Send for You'—John Fox and the Medal of Honor." The National Medal of Honor Museum. February 19, 2021. https://mohmuseum.org/john-fox-and-the-medal-of-honor/; National Park Services. n.d. "John R. Fox (U.S. National Park Service)." n.d. NPS .gov. Accessed May 23, 2023. https://www.nps.gov/people/johnfox.htm; The National WWII Museum. 2020. "African Americans Fought for Freedom at Home and Abroad During World War II." The National WWII Museum, New Orleans. February 1, 2020. https://www.nationalww2museum.org/war/articles/african-americans-fought-freedom-home-and-abroad-during-world-war-ii#:~: text=Article-.

213 *As part of a study* Achor, Shawn, Andrew Reece, Gabriella Kellerman, and Alexi Robichaux. 2018. "9 out of 10 People Are Willing to Earn Less Money to Do More-Meaningful Work." *Harvard Business Review.* November 6, 2018. https://hbr.org/2018/11/9-out-of-10-people-are-willing-to-earn-less-money-to-do-more-meaningful-work.

213 *Unfortunately, according to research* Gallup Inc. n.d. "How to Measure Employee Engagement with the Q12." Gallup. https://www.gallup.com/workplace/356045/q12-question-summary.aspx.

216 *Research conducted by Adam Grant* Grant, Adam. *Give and Take: Why Helping Others Drives Our Success.* New York: Penguin Books, 2014.

221 *In fact, this is* Sinek, Simon. 2014. "Why Good Leaders Make You Feel Safe." TED Talks. May 19, 2014. Video, 11:46. https://www.ted.com/talks/simon_sinek_why_good_leaders_make_you_feel_safe/c.

ABOUT THE AUTHOR

Matt Tenney envisions a world in which all leaders and workplace cultures consistently make a positive impact on the well-being and growth of team members.

Since 2012—as an author, consultant, and trainer—Matt has delivered programs that develop highly effective leaders who improve employee engagement, performance, and retention to hundreds of clients, including many Fortune 500 companies.

Matt is also frequently invited to deliver keynote speeches at conferences. He is known for giving inspiring, thought-provoking keynote speeches and has served a wide range of clients, including the Credit Union National Association, the American Society for Association Executives, the Corporate Housing Providers Association, the American Dental Association, and many other state and national associations and conferences.

When he's not traveling for speaking or consulting engagements, Matt can be found in Nashville, TN.

To connect with Matt, please visit www.MattTenney.com.